Batteries Not Included

ROBERT BERINGER

SERMONS FOR THE
SUNDAYS AFTER PENTECOST
(SUNDAYS IN ORDINARY TIME)
FIRST THIRD

CYCLE C GOSPEL TEXTS

C.S.S. Publishing Co., Inc.

Lima, Ohio

BATTERIES NOT INCLUDED

Library of Congress Cataloging-in-Publication Data

Beringer, Robert, 1936-
    Batteries not included.

    Bibliography: p.
    1. Church year sermons. 2. Sermons, American. I. Title.
BV4253.B43   1988   252'.6   88-2894
ISBN 1-55673-055-1

8852 / ISBN 1-55673-055-1

Table of Contents

[1]Common Lectionary
[2]Lutheran Lectionary
[3]Roman Catholic Lectionary

In Gratitude

To

Peggy, David, Peter, Beth, and Tom

And for all they have taught
me about the power of our God

Introduction

Did you ever buy one of those toys that moves by itself, because it is powered by a battery? You push the button and it moves, or runs, or cries. Often you get it home, full of anticipation of a child's joy when they push that "start" button, only to read the fine print for the first time and discover, "batteries not included."

The gift of life does not come with batteries included. That's the small print on the package. You have to decide to add the power. You can choose to live without power, just as a child can go on playing with a toy whose batteries are no longer working. Millions of people in our time have chosen to live that way — without the power and the help our gracious Creator intends for us to have. They often "get by," but they miss the opportunity to experience life in all its fulness and joy, as God intended it.

That great Episcopal leader, Sam Shoemaker, wrote years ago, "I am perfectly sure that spiritual power is as available to us as electricity. It is about us all the time, waiting to be appropriated. The air is filled with it." Yet too many of the followers of Christ have never experienced that power in their daily living. They live lives in a ho-hum, "country-club-esque" Christianity, never knowing the power, the companionship, or the help that Christ promised to his followers through the gift of the Holy Spirit.

The messages which follow deal largely with the themes of power and faith. They are messages for those who have discovered that batteries are not included in life, and who long to live power-filled lives. God has promised to empower you to live as a Christian in a way you never thought possible. But you and I must take the initiative in accepting the gift that God offers each one of us through the power of the Holy Spirit. My prayer is that these sermons will help you to become a powerful person, full of his Holy Spirit.

Robert Beringer

Lectionary Preaching After Pentecost

Virtually all pastors who make use of the sermons in this book will find their worship life and planning shaped by one of two lectionary series. Most mainline Protestant denominations, along with clergy of the Roman Catholic Church, have now approved — either for provisional or official use — the three-year Common (Consensus) Lectionary. This family of denominations includes United Methodist, Presbyterian, United Church of Christ, and Disciples of Christ.

Lutherans and Roman Catholics, while testing the Common Lectionary on a limited basis at present, follow their own three-year cycle of texts. While there are divergences between the Common and Lutheran/Roman Catholic systems, the gospel texts show striking parallels, with few text selections evidencing significant differences. Virtually all the gospel texts included in this book will, therefore, be applicable to worship and preaching planning for clergy following either lectionary.

A significant divergence does occur, however, in the method by which specific gospel texts are assigned to specific calendar days. The Common and Roman Catholic lectionaries accomplish this by counting backwards from Christ the King (Last Sunday after Pentecost), discarding "extra" texts from the front of the list; Lutherans follow the opposite pattern, counting forward from The Holy Trinity, discarding "extra" texts at the end of the list.

The following index will aid the user of this book in matching the right text to the right Sunday during the "Pentecost Half" of the church year (days listed here include only those appropriate to this book's contents):

Fixed Date Lectionaries   **Lutheran Lectionary**

Text Designation

Common   *Roman Catholic*

The Day of   The Day of   The Day of
Pentecost   Pentecost   Pentecost

8

The Holy Trinity	The Holy Trinity	The Holy Trinity
Proper 4 *May 29-June 4*	Ordinary Time 9	Pentecost 2
Proper 5 *June 5-11*	Ordinary Time 10	Pentecost 3
Proper 6 *June 12-18*	Ordinary Time 11	Pentecost 4
Proper 7 *June 19-25*	Ordinary Time 12	Pentecost 5
Proper 8 *June 26 — July 2*	Ordinary Time 13	Pentecost 6
Proper 9 *July 3-9*	Ordinary Time 14	Pentecost 7

Promises, Promises!

Dr. A. Leonard Griffith, the former pastor of the City Temple in London, asks us to imagine a race of uncivilized, savage people, living far back in the jungles of South America. One day a missionary doctor comes to their village, and by sheer miracle they do not kill him, but allow him to minister to them in the name of Jesus Christ. His powers of healing seem to them godlike. He makes a tremendous impact on those primitive people in healing them of diseases they had always regarded as fatal. In time he learns their language, and some of the natives, knowing that this stranger cares about them deeply, respond to his message about God's love and mercy in Christ. They form a kind of primitive church in the jungle.

The day comes, however, when the missionary doctor announces that he must leave and return to his own country. The natives cannot contain their sorrow. This surely means the end of everything. Tearfully the little band of Christians gathers on the eve of the doctor's departure to bid him farewell. But the doctor astonishes them with a promise that life will be better for them because he is going home! He explains that his own period of service was never intended to be more than temporary. He has come to them as a pioneer, to begin the Christian work in their community. His return home will make it possible for the mission board to send a permanent minister, one who will live with them and remain with them, who will preach the same Gospel, lead them into a deeper understanding of it, and help them to share their new faith with others.[1]

Such was the promise made by Jesus on the eve of his crucifixion to his own sorrowing disciples. By his works of healing and redemption, Jesus had made a tremendous impact. He had gathered around him a group of followers who never thought of themselves apart from him. Now he was about to leave them! They would be on their own! How could they possibly carry on without him? Five times in that Upper Room Jesus assures his fearful disciples that they will never be alone — that he will send them a Companion, a representative who will remain with them permanently and who will teach them all they need to know to share the story of God's amazing grace with the world.

In that same Upper Room the Master's promise came mightily to fulfillment. Something took possession of the disciples at Pentecost, something that brought them to know Jesus as they had never known him throughout his earthly ministry. They felt his presence with them, his active, pulsating presence inspiring them with a boldness, a confidence, an enthusiasm that changed them from a disorganized, dispirited group of men and women into a radiant, world-conquering fellowship! What exactly did Jesus promise to his followers, both then and now, that can transform our lives as it once did to those who felt alone and powerless? A study of John's Gospel finds the Master promising us four gifts:

1. A Living Companion

First, there is the promise of a Living Companion. Just as the missionary doctor promised those South American natives another representative from the home country, so Jesus promised his followers that another representative from God would come to take his place. Now notice that Jesus did not say of the Spirit, *"it"* will guide you into all truth. He said, *"he"* will guide you into all truth. It was as if Jesus was saying, "My personal representative will be right there beside you, no matter what happens.

The promise of Christ's presence with us, however, is a hard one for us to understand. I think of the man who got on a plane to Chicago and found himself seated next to a Roman Catholic nun. However, the nun was shaking so much that neither of them could get comfortably seated. The man watched the nun wringing her hands, and finally asked her why she was so nervous. The nun quickly explained that this was her first airplane flight ever and she was frightened to death at the prospect. Her seat companion sought to calm her fears by saying, "Sister, you do believe that God is with you always, don't you?" And grabbing his hand in hers, the frightened nun replied, "Yes, I guess so. But remember: he said, 'And *low*, I am with you always!' " Like that nun, many of us feel it would have been a lot easier to understand Jesus and believe in him if only we had known him in the days of his flesh. If we had felt the magnetism of his personality, if we had listened to his teaching with our own ears, and watched his healing the sick and the infirm with our own eyes, we would have no doubts whatsoever. We want it as the familiar hymn puts it:

> *I think when I read that sweet story of old,*
> *When Jesus was here among men,*
> *How he called little children as lambs to his fold,*
> *I should like to have been with him then.*

But supposing we had been with Jesus in the first century. Would we really have understood him any better? Did the disciples in the first century come closer to the truth about God because they walked the roads of Galilee with God's own Son? It is a curious fact of our human experience that we sometimes feel closer to a person's true spirit after they have gone away from us. A child romps about the house getting on her parents' nerves but not always into their understanding. Then, when that precious young voice is stilled by death, and the step is no longer heard on the stairs, those parents have the light of recognition breaking forth in their minds, and they begin to see their daughter in all her fulness.

Something like that happened to Jesus' own disciples at Pentecost. Suddenly they grasped the fact that the Jesus who was now present with them as the Spirit, was a companion who was free to go wherever they could go, to share their joys and their sorrows in a way no earthly, flesh-bound friend ever could. To agnostics and unbelievers, this promise of a Living Companion will sound like utter nonsense. To a person who knows nothing of astronomy, there will be nothing unusual in the night sky. To a person who knows nothing of art, there will be nothing significant in a Rembrandt painting. But to the person who is open to God's breaking into life in all the fulness of his presence, there is a Living Companion who can help us to face even the worst that life can bring. Jesus said of the Spirit, "But you know him, for he dwells with you, and will be with you."

In the 1950s there was a popular radio announcer by the name of Ted Husing. He suddenly dropped out of the picture because he had to undergo a brain operation. It left him blind, paralyzed, and unable to speak. Like many of us when the bottom drops out of life, Ted Husing became bitter in his suffering. He refused to see anyone except his wife and daughter. However, some old Christian friends would not give up on Ted Husing. They kept coming to see him, praying for him and encouraging him. He could not understand their patience or their stubbornness. At last Ted allowed one friend to take him to a baseball game where at least he could hear the crack of the bat and smell the heavenly odor of hot dogs and peanuts. During the game, Ted's friend whispered to him, "Ted, you are going to make it with the help of God. You may think you face this illness all alone, but the thousands of people who are praying for you every day, all across this country, know something you have forgotten. They know that God is in this with you, all the way.!"[2] Ted Husing often said that the simple faith of this good friend was what restored his own confidence in a loving God who was with him, even in his darkness. That is the promise of a Living Companion who is always with us.

2. A Living Teacher

But Christ also promised his sorrowing disciples a Living Teacher. How little the disciples understood of their Master's teaching! How little they grasped of the essential meaning of his relationship to God and the work of salvation that he and the Father were to accomplish on the Cross! They were not supermen; they possessed only average intelligence. But Jesus, being a wise teacher, did not overwhelm his pupils with an avalanche of facts they could not grasp. Instead, he led them forward, step by step, until that night in the Upper Room where he said, "I have many things to say to you, but you cannot bear them now. When the Spirit of Truth comes, he will guide you into all the truth . . . he will take what is mine and declare it to you." And down through the centuries, the followers of Christ have known this Spirit of Truth that has led them into an ever deeper and richer understanding of the truth in Jesus Christ.

It was Martin Luther who said that the simple scullery maid studying the Bible with the help of the Holy Spirit can come closer to the truth about God than the greatest scholar studying without the help of the Holy Spirit. Why is it that the faith of some of the most sophisticated and well-educated people crumbles under the impact of suffering while the faith of some humble folk seems to surmount the most discouraging obstacles? The answer would seem to be that these latter folk have a Teacher in the Christian life, one who trains them and interprets all of life for them in such a way that they can deal with whatever difficulties may come their way.

Dr. Mary Verghese, an Indian woman, qualified as an orthopedic surgeon at Vellore Christian Medical College back in the early 50s. Two years later, however, an automobile accident crippled her for life. Doctors had to break the tragic news that not only would she never walk again, but that from her arms downwards, she would never feel again and never move again. This young Indian woman, took the news with hardly a word. Instead, she asked a friend to read from the Scriptures for her daily, and continued to believe that God would teach her what his purpose would be for what remained of her life. She never doubted that God had something for her to do in medical work.

She became interested in leprosy patients, because at that time a French surgeon had perfected a technique for grafting tendons and transforming the wasted stumps of lepers into something like hands and feet. At her own insistence Mary Verghese underwent three long operations which resulted in her being able to sit upright in a wheelchair. Then she began to specialize all over again. By the 1960s she was back in the operating room at Vellore, doing hand and foot reconstructions, performing surgery from a wheelchair. Almost as important as the work itself is the encouragement her patients receive by seeing someone who is even more paralyzed than they are, using her life to help others. Mary Verghese is a Christian who met the worst life could bring her, in the confidence that a Living Teacher would open a whole new chapter in God's purpose for her life. That was exactly what Jesus promised.

3. A Living Authority

Thirdly, our Lord promised that his followers would have a Living Authority who would guide them in their walk of faith. This was the critical problem faced by Jesus' disciples. He had called them to share in his ministry of teaching and healing and reconciliation, and so long as he remained with them, they knew what to do, where to go and how to serve. But with him gone, they felt like ships adrift on the ocean without a chart or a compass.

And is that not our problem as well, as we face difficult choices and demanding decisions in our daily walk with Christ?[2] Sometimes we wish this promise of the Holy Spirit meant that we had a direct line to heaven, so that we could hear the voice of our Lord telling us what to do. In one of our national magazines there appeared the story of a Christian congregation, one of whose members was a surgeon at the local hospital. He was active in the life of the church. He was also affiliated with Holy Spirit Hospital. Like many doctors, he carried a beeper attached to his belt so that he could be contacted at any time. But some in the congregation wondered if he had a special line to the Lord when, during a service, a voice on his beeper loudly announced: "Dr. Fricke, call Holy Spirit!"

Usually, however, the guidance of God's Spirit does not come to us over a beeper. But that does not mean for a moment that the Spirit is not authoritatively giving direction to our lives. In the Acts of the Apostles, we see many specific instances of God's guidance in the career of the Apostle Paul. When Paul and his companions were about to push north into Asia Minor, Luke tells us that the Spirit of God prevented them. The same Spirit spoke through Paul's dream, beckoning those first Christian missionaries in the direction of Europe. This was exactly what Jesus promised — a living authority who would guide his followers in every age concerning how they should act in obedience to their Lord.

As a young man, Abraham Lincoln went to the Black Hawk War a captain, and, through no fault of his own, returned a private. That brought an end to his military career. Then his little shop in a country village "winked out," as he used to say, marking his failure as a businessman. As a lawyer in Springfield, he was too impractical, too unpolished, and too tempermental to be a success. Turning to politics (and some people feel that is where folks turn when all else fails!), Abraham Lincoln was defeated in his first attempt to be nominated for Congress, defeated in his application to be a Commissioner to the General Land Office, defeated in the senatorial Election of 1854, defeated for the Vice-Presidency in 1856, defeated again in the senatorial Election of 1858. Yet in 1861, Lincoln found himself sitting in the White House as President of the United States! How did he interpret this strange succession of failures and frustrations which finally culminated in the Presidency? This is what he wrote: "That Almighty God directly intervenes in human affairs is one of the plainest statements in the Bible. I have had so many evidences of his direction, so many instances when I have been controlled by some other Power than my own will, that I have no doubt but what this Power comes from above."[3] This is the gift of a Living Authority whose guidance often conflicts with our own will, but who can lead us into a fulness of understanding and obedience to Christ that we will find nowhere else in life.

4. A Living Helper

Finally, our Lord promised his disciples a Living Helper. Bible scholars differ in their translations of the Greek word *paracletos*, the term Jesus used to describe the Spirit. In some versions, the Spirit is called a "Comforter," a "Counselor," and an "Advocate." William Barclay tells us that the word literally means "someone who is called in to help us," such as a lawyer called in to plead a difficult case, or an expert called in to give advice in a difficult situation. No one can set out on the walk of faith in this world without quickly discovering just how precious this promise is! Something rekindles the fires of hope and keeps men and women working for God, even when the world makes a mockery of their faith. It is the Helper, the Living Spirit of God who comes beside us in our despair to brace us up, to revive our faith, and to be the strength we do not possess within ourselves to withstand evil.

Sometimes we miss this Living Helper, because we forget that God's living Spirit works through other people. A man named Smith was sitting on his roof during a flood, and the water was up to his feet. Before long a man in a canoe paddled past, and shouted, "Can I give you a lift to higher ground?'' ''No thanks,'' said Smith. ''I have faith in the Lord and he will save me.''

Soon the water rose to Smith's waist. At this point a motor boat pulled up, and a woman called out, ''Can I give you a lift to higher ground?'' ''No thanks,'' said Smith. ''I have faith in the Lord and he will help me.'' Later a helicopter flew by, and Smith who was now standing on the roof with the water up to his neck, heard a voice say, ''Grab the rope, and I'll pull you up.'' ''No thanks,'' said Smith. ''I have faith in the Lord and he will help me.'' But after hours of treading water, Smith drowned and went to his reward in heaven. As he arrived, Smith said to the Lord, ''I had such faith in you to save me and you let me down. What happened?'' To which the Lord replied, ''What do you want from me? I sent you two boats and a helicopter!'' Sometimes we have missed the help God desires to give us, because we have not really yielded control of our lives in faith and obedience to his Living Spirit. But God wants to give us spiritual power. He wants us to continue the ministry begun by Christ, not in our own strength, but with his strength. And that is why Jesus Christ promised his followers long ago, and even those of us who follow him now, that he would send us a Living Helper.

One of those special people whom God has used to enrich my faith and life is a blind woman who lived in New Jersy for many years. Her name is Annie Johnson Flint, and her poems of faith have often ministered to some deep hurts in my life. In the darkness of her blindness, this young woman discovered the reality of the Helper Christ promised long ago in the Upper Room. She has written:

> *He giveth more grace when the burdens grow greater,*
> *He sendeth more strength when the labors increase;*
> *To added affliction He addeth His mercy*
> *To multiplied trials, His multiplied peace.*

> *When we have exhausted our store of endurance,*
> *When our strength has failed and the day is half done,*
> *When we reach the end of our hoarded resources,*
> *Our Father's full giving is only begun.*

His love has no limit, His grace has no measure;
His power no boundary known unto men;
For out of His infinite riches in Jesus
He giveth and giveth and giveth again.[4]

Promises, promises! Let us rejoice on this Day of Pentecost in the God who keeps his promises and sends to us a Living Companion, A Living Teacher, A Living Authority and a Living Helper.

John 15:26-27; 16:4b-11   *The Day of Pentecost (Lutheran)*

Help Available!

All over the world today there is a growing interest, in churches both large and small, in the work of the Holy Spirit. According to Catherine Marshall, in her popular book, *The Helper*, "There is no greater need in the church today than to be informed about the helper, to know who he is, and why we need him in our lives."[1] For many of us who have grown up in the church, there has been little taught or said about the Holy Spirit. My Sunday church school teachers spent long hours talking about God the Father, and Christ the Savior, but almost nothing was ever said about the Holy Spirit. It reminds me of the old story of the church that was never satisfied with its preacher. Each year, the bishop sent a new preacher to that church, and each year the officers came back and asked the bishop for a change of pastors. Finally, the bishop sent an elderly man with a fading memory and a faltering voice to be their preacher. The next year, the officers came back and told the bishop that this man would do just fine for another year. "How come you want this pastor when I have sent you so many fine ones that did not work out?" asked the bishop. "Well sir, you know that we really would prefer to have no preacher at all, and this old man we have now is the nearest to nothing we have ever had!"

Until recent years in many churches, the Holy Spirit has meant little or nothing to most members. But the wind of God is blowing with new freshness in many congregations, and

Christians are learning that the Holy Spirit, the Helper, is the One who makes it possible for ordinary, garden-variety disciples to live new lives in Jesus Christ. A more careful study of the Gospels has revealed the fact that our Lord never intended his disciples to live the Christian life in their own strength. Not only did the Risen Christ promise his power, but in John's Gospel, he promises One who will be a Counselor who will "convince the world of sin and of righteousness and of judgment." That means there is help available, God's help, for every single person who makes a commitment to follow Jesus Christ.

No one has ever found living the Christian life an easy task. Look at the life of the Apostle Paul. Never was any man more conscious of his own weakness — that gulf between what he wanted to accomplish for Christ, and what in fact he was able to do. Paul was ready to give up on many occasions, but over and over again when he reached that point where his human resources failed, there seemed to surge through him a strength from beyond that nerved him and kept him going. That's how Paul understood the work of God's Spirit, as the One "who helps us in our weakness." The truth we ponder on Pentecost is that we have a helper in the Christian life, the Spirit of the Living Christ, who reaches out to us in every area of weakness in our lives. Let us consider the help that is available to us.

1. Help for Our Intellectual Weakness

The Spirit of truth can help us deal with the reality of doubt in our lives. I once knew a minister who had many gifts, a good mind, a warm personality, and a fine speaking voice. He had every ingredient for success, except for one thing — he could never come to terms with his doubts. He studied, he wrestled, he listened to great teachers, he read all the right books, but still he stumbled over some doctrines and one Sunday morning, he shocked his congregation by saying: "I don't know what I believe and I don't believe half of what I say.

I have no alternative, therefore, but to leave the ministry." And he did! I have always admired that pastor's honesty, but I cannot help wondering if he did not make the mistake many Christians make in struggling with their doubts all by themselves. After all, no one can hope to understand the whole truth of God! The finite mind simply cannot comprehend the infinite.

Moreover, whoever said we have to swallow the whole of Christian dogma in one gulp? Even to the disciples who had been with Jesus day and night, he had to say in the Upper Room, "I have many things to say to you, but you cannot bear them now." Divine truth comes slowly, and if those first disciples are any example for us, it is clear that truth comes not through a lot of spinning of our human wheels, but as the Spirit of God teaches us in the rough and tumble of everyday life. I have often met people with little or no formal education who possess a profound understanding of Christian truth. Only one explanation is possible: God has given them their understanding! As Martin Luther summed it up, "The simple scullery maid with the Holy Spirit can know more of God than the greatest scholar without the Holy Spirit."

That pastor who left the ministry because of his doubts is today employed by IBM Corporation in Texas. It was only after he left the ministry that he was introduced to the Helper, the Counselor. Those unanswerable doubts and questions became manageable when he was helped to face his own intellectual weakness, and to seek the help of the Living Christ. I thank God for that man in my own life, because more than anyone else, he has helped me to rediscover the work of the Holy Spirit in my walk of faith.

2. Help for our Devotional Weakness

Many Christians feel inadequate when it comes to the area of their personal devotional lives. There is perhaps nothing more difficult in the Christian life than the discipline of prayer. Often just the plain human need for sleep overcomes us, just as it overcame the disciples in the Garden of Gethsemane. Someone once asked Cardinal Spellman if, with all the work he did in a day, he ever got so tired, he forgot to say his prayers at night. The Cardinal, with a wink of his eye, said, "Oh, no!" When I am so tired that I cannot keep my eyes open, I just say, "Dear God, you know I've been working in your vineyard all day. If you don't mind, can we skip the details until morning?"

When it comes to praying, some of us, unfortunately, skip the details for a lot longer than a single night! And who of us has not felt that even when we *do* manage to articulate our longings, there is always that nagging doubt that no one hears them anyway! Too often we have had the experience of praying, and yet nothing seems to happen. But that is precisely the point where the Spirit helps us in our weakness. Many times something or someone keeps drawing us back again to the secret place. Someone keeps beckoning us to get on our knees once more and open our hearts to the Lord. In an even more profound way, many of us have experienced times when petitions of almost sublime spiritual insight have poured forth from our lips, almost as if another were speaking through us. The words are ours, yet not ours, as we have prayed from the depth of our hearts for someone in need. Praying becomes a whole different experience when, instead of praying in our own strength, we come before God with surrendered hearts, knowing our human weakness, and knowing that the Helper can draw us closer to God and his love than anything we could ever do in our human strength and wisdom.

In the town where I once served as pastor, there was a remarkable man who served as a deacon in his black Baptist Church. Bob was a humble person who had little or no formal education. He had terrible problems with his health, and yet had to work very hard all his life. But when this simple Christian stood before his congregation and said, "Let us pray," the language of devotion that flowed from him was like a beautiful symphony that transported everyone to the gates of heaven. It was as if something possessed him, as if the Spirit of God within him was speaking to God above. That is the help God offers to you and me in our prayer lives, the Spirit of the Living Christ within us appealing to the Father above on our behalf.

3. Help for Our Moral Weakness

In the everyday struggle to discern right from wrong, who of us has not failed miserably? We know what Christ requires of us. We know in every situation there is a Christlike thing to do, a Christian way to react, a Christian word to say, and a Christian decision to make. And yet in our hearts, we know as well how often we have been weak and afraid. There was once a businessman telling a friend how important it was to have Christian ethics in his business. "Why just the other day an old customer paid his account with a hundred dollar bill. As he was leaving, I discovered that he had mistakenly handed me two hundreds, stuck together. Immediately the question of Christian ethics arose: Should I tell my boss about the other hundred or not?"

We need little reminder that we have failed our Lord morally on many occasions. Can it be that here, also, we have made the mistake of going it all alone? After all, our walk with the living Christ is not a system of ethics. It's a Gospel, it's good news of something that God causes to happen in us by his love and grace. When the New Testament talks about the fruit of the Christian life as being love, joy, peace, gentleness, goodness, faith, meekness and temperance, it does not suggest that these are like merit badges we achieve by our own efforts. Rather it describes these qualities as the *gifts* of the Helper, the things only God can give to those with a yielded heart. In other words, these are qualities we cannot cultivate. We can only pray for them. We cannot achieve them. We can only receive them as God's gifts.

That truth is dramatically illustrated in the life of Francis of Assisi. Francis had been a self-seeking dilettante before surrendering his heart to Christ. He himself tells of how repulsed he was by the sight of lepers — those uncared-for outcasts of humanity. One day Francis met a leper. He was about to spur his horse on when his fear and disgust gave way to an urgent impulse to dismount from his horse and embrace the leper. Slowly and deliberately he pressed the man's rotten flesh against his lips. It was in that moment that the figure he was embracing seemed to him to become the figure of Jesus Christ himself! You simply cannot love like that in your own strength! But with the Helper, incredible strength comes to us at the point of our greatest moral weakness.

Many years ago, two women came to America for a Christian conference. It was soon after the Second World War. One woman, Mrs. Uemura, was from Japan. The other, Dr. Llano, was from the Philippines. Both were Christians, and both arrived separately in this country. They met for the first time at breakfast one morning. When the Philippine woman saw the Japanese woman, visions of her own country, her home, her family, her hospital — all devastated by the Japanese soldiers — flashed through her memory. She could not even say a word to this Japanese woman, and she abruptly turned and left the room. However, on the last morning of the Conference, the Japanese woman heard a knock on her door. She opened it to find Dr. Llano, the Philippine woman, standing there. With tears in her eyes she said to Mrs. Uemura: "I have sought God's forgiveness for the way I treated you, but I can have no peace in my heart until I ask your forgiveness as well." Then it was the Japanese lady's turn to cry, and finally she put her arms around the Philippine woman and said, "And can you ever forgive what my people did to your people in the War?"[2] Together the women prayed. Then after washing their faces, they went to breakfast together, having experienced what only the Helper, the Spirit of God, can do to help us in our moral weakness.

4. Help for Our Redemptive Weakness

I have a feeling that the most serious source of discouragement in the Christian life is the suspicion that we are really not Christians at all. We have always been aware that a vital faith adds up to more than correct theology, more than devotional discipline, and more than good moral character. Beyond that, we have a sense that something is supposed to happen in us — something radical and redemptive that changes our personalities. We yearn to have the experience that Jesus spoke about to Nicodemus on the night when he said, "You must be born again." But though we have yearned with all our hearts for such a dramatic experience with the Lord, it simply has never happened to us.

Once more I suggest that we have made the mistake of trying to write the script of our lives without any help from God. Too many of us, myself included for many years, have sought to live a new life in Christ, without ever realizing that it is God and God alone who brings us into a saving relationship with his Son. A lot of us continue to repeat the experience of Luther who, even as a Christian monk, ran the whole gamut of the Roman Catholic penitential system and engaged in every form of religious discipline, only to discover in his moment of greatest frustration that "the just shall live by faith," and not by anything that we do within ourselves. There are two factors in a vital redemptive experience. There is God's gracious act in Christ, and there is our human response of faith and trust and obedience. "By grace are ye saved, through faith; and that — *even that* — not of yourselves: it is the gift of God."

Dean Ernest Gordon, now retired from the Princeton University Chapel, tells us in one of his books how the Spirit of Jesus Christ helps us in our redemptive need. Gordon was a prisoner of war of the Japanese. He described how the men in his POW camp were degraded, starved, tortured and reduced to the status of animals by their captors. Every man's hand was against his neighbor's. These prisoners cursed, hated, stole from one another, and watched each other die without hope.

In desperation, Gordon and a few others formed a group to read from the Bible. Over many weeks there occurred a kind of spiritual awakening in the midst of their jungle hell. Inspired by the few who had come to know Christ as their Savior, others joined their group and began to seek his help. They formed what Gordon says was a "church of the Spirit." He explains: "It had to be the Spirit that transformed the life of that camp, for men suddenly began helping one another to live. Where there had been darkness, now there was hope. Where men had hated each other, now there was love." As Gordon summed it up, "This change was not merely a rosy glow in the abdomen; it was a literal in-breathing of the Holy Spirit, for we had nowhere else to turn in our desperate weakness, except to the Lord."[3]

A Church Of The Spirit — I just wonder what might happen across America if you and I and the rest of God's people could admit our weakness, and open our hearts to the Helper, who is none other than the Living Christ? Help is available! The question this day is: Do we have the *faith* to believe and the *courage* to act?

The Wind Of God

The focus of our worship on Pentecost is the gift of God's Holy Spirit, and yet there are few subjects about which the average Christian feels more uncertain. For many people, the mere mention of the Holy Ghost conjures up an image of a mysterious figure dressed in ethereal white, one who haunts cemeteries, old houses, and even old churches. I have always loved the story of the two little boys who went to a Sunday church service for the first time, and witnessed a baptism. They listened carefully to the whole proceeding, and decided as children often do, to repeat the whole performance that afternoon in the backyard. One of them dug a hole in the ground, filled it with water, and brought the family dog to the edge of the hole. Then the "minister" said: "I baptize you in the name of the Father, and of the Son," and then after a moment's hesitation, he added, "and in the hole he goes." With that the two boys shoved the dog into the drink!

For a lot of people, until quite recently, that was all they knew about the Holy Ghost. But fortunately, you and I are privileged to be living in a time when Christians all over the world are rediscovering the importance of the Holy Spirit. It is a rediscovery that God not only worked in the lives of ancient people like Abraham and Sarah, and the prophets, or that in a moment of time, the Spirit of God entered into the life of Jesus of Nazareth in a unique way. What has captured the imagination and the hearts of Christians in almost every church is a conviction that God is doing the same things that he did long ago in the lives of people today. This is a God who renews, empowers, and directs our lives through his Holy Spirit. This is a God who is active in the present tense, and desires to fill your life and mine with his power and blessing.

Let me be quite personal about this rediscovery. I realized some years ago that in my own walk with Christ, I had long had the *philosophy* of Jesus in my head. I understood the *program* of Jesus for the world. But what I lacked was the *power* of Jesus to live out each day in obedience to the Lord. I was trying desperately to love, to serve, to minister and to forgive all in my own strength. The result was a terrible sense of frustration and doubt about my calling as a pastor. Then my eyes were opened to one of the central messages of the Bible, a truth expressed in a thousand of our hymns and in all of our creeds. That truth is that God himself gives us the power to preach, to witness, to teach, to heal, to love and even to forgive through his Holy Spirit. I can honestly tell you that rediscovering the Holy Spirit has changed both my life and my ministry.

Why is this rediscovery of the third person of the Trinity taking place? I think the answer is that many people today yearn for a warm, sustaining, and exciting faith — a faith that is more than cold mental assent to a bunch of doctrines or dogmas. They desire a faith that is more than a feverish running after good causes and good works, so that we can somehow earn our way into heaven. People seem hungry for a faith that works from within, that transcends denominational barriers and that offers spiritual power beyond the resources of this secular world. In short, people want to experience the power, the freedom, and the joy that Christ promised to his disciples in the Upper Room long ago.

What does the Holy Spirit actually do in our lives? I think we are helped in answering that question by remembering John's account of that post-Easter visit of the Lord with his disciples. You will recall that John says of Jesus, "He breathed

on them and said, 'Receive the Holy Spirit.' " In Hebrew and
in Greek, the word for spirit is always associated with wind
or breath. I know of no better way of understanding the work
of the Holy Spirit than to use the Bible's own imagery which
represents the Holy Spirit as the refreshing, re-invigorating,
recreating breath of God. It is no accident that the account
given in the Acts of the Apostles of that first Pentecost includes the fact that this gift of God was given "with the rush
of a mighty wind."
But we can hear it and feel its force, and certainly we can look
upon its effects. When the ancient Hebrews thought of the in-
visible God, and his effect on their lives, they likened his
presence to the wind which sometimes could devastate their
land with gale force, and at other times be that blessed, refreshing breeze that made life possible for a wilderness people. Let's
think together about some of the things that wind or breath
does in our lives.

1. A Sign Of Life

Breath is a sign of life. If you stop breathing, you stop living! Even our marvelous computers and mechanical brains do
not breathe. Only the Spirit of God gives breath to our physical bodies, and I have come to believe that it is that same Holy
Spirit which breathes new life into us when we invite Jesus
Christ to be the Lord and Savior of our lives. I can recall being astounded and amazed at the birth of our two children
when I was allowed to be present in the delivery room. To witness that miracle of life, the birth of a living, breathing infant,
is a tremendous experience. But no less a miracle than human
birth is the miracle that God works in our lives when we are
reborn and made new in the image of Christ. The Apostle Paul
describes that new life by saying that the Spirit of Christ within us produces fruit in our lives, and those fruits are: love,
joy, peace, patience, kindness, gentleness and self-control. But
Paul never thought for a moment that we made Christians out

of our own efforts. The Christian life is not a cultivating of the Christian graces, or manicuring our souls, or even a pulling up of ourselves by our own moral bootstraps. Rather, you and I can change and become different persons only when we permit the cleansing and renewing wind of God's Spirit to gain entrance to our hearts.

Let me suggest that the Spirit of God brings new life to us in two ways. First, it is the Spirit that convicts us of our own sinfulness. A new piece of furniture in a room often makes you realize how shabby the rest of the furniture has become. A chance swipe of a mechanic's rag on the hood of your car lets you know how dirty the car has become. I believe that something like that happens when a person allows their heart to be touched by the Spirit of Christ. You begin to listen to your own conscience, to measure your life not against what is acceptable to your crowd, but against the life of Jesus. It is then that you find yourself convicted inwardly of your own selfishness, your rebelliousness against the law of God and your own emptiness in trying to live life without God.

There was once an African man who, along with many others, was watching a film shown by a missionary. The film depicted the life of Jesus. The African was held in rapt attention until finally, when they came to the Crucifixion scene, he suddenly got up and ran towards the movie screen. Falling down in front of the picture of Christ suffering on the Cross, he shouted tearfully, "Oh Jesus, come down from your Cross; it is me who should be hanging there, not you!" That is the working of God's Spirit that convicts us of our own sinfulness.

However, the Spirit not only convicts but convinces us to accept God's offer of forgiveness and love. Wind has often been a life-changing force when it blows across the landscape. The new wind that blows in our lives when Christ is allowed to take control of our hearts is a force that can change our lives from top to bottom, and convince us, as no other power on earth, of the truth we have seen in Jesus. A story from the Second World War illustrates how powerfully the Spirit of God can change the hearts of people. A Nazi platoon entered a village on the edge of the Argonne Forest. Snipers from the village fired and killed six of the German soldiers. A search was made by the Germans, but no snipers were found. The Lieutenant in charge immediately ordered the arrest of six civilians picked at random who were taken away and sentenced to die at dawn of the following day by a firing squad. That night the village priest went to visit the condemned men. One of them was a young man who wept and begged the priest to intercede with the German officer on behalf of his wife and four children. The priest found the Lieutenant, and quietly said, "Sir, this prisoner is young and has a family. I am old and have no one. It can make no difference to you which of us dies in the morning. Let me take this young man's place." With utter contempt, the officer looked at the priest and said, "You are a fool! If you want to die, go ahead and take his place."

But later that night the young officer filed a report by field telephone of the whole incident, including the priest's taking the place of the young father. That report came to the attention of the commanding general who found himself deeply moved by the self-sacrifice of the priest. All that night the general wrestled with his conscience as he heard Jesus saying, "Greater love has no man than this, that a man lay down his life for his friend." Early in the morning the General sent word to let all six of the prisoners go free.[1] Once again, not human ingenuity but the power of God's life-giving Spirit had changed a man's heart and convinced him that there was another way. It was this power to change human lives that the old hymnwriter celebrated when he wrote: "Breathe on me, breath of God. Fill me with life anew, that I may love as Thou didst love, and do that Thou wouldst do."

2. A Sign Of Power

Wind or breath is also a sign of power. For generations people have harnessed the power of the wind to sail ships, to turn windmills, and to carry airplanes aloft. Ask any athlete about breath supply, and they will tell you how important it is to get that "second wind" when you are in the midst of the race. In like fashion, the writers of the Bible saw God's empowering of his people as being like the forces of the wind. The Bible is the record of how ordinary people just like us become spiritual giants when the Spirit of God breathed a power into their lives that helped them turn the world upside down for Christ. This is not just willpower, or positive thinking, or even the power that sometimes comes to us in a moment of great fear.

A boy was sent to the store by his mother after dark. He decided to cut through the cemetery on his way to the store, but he failed to see the open grave and suddenly he found himself trapped in the hole. It was raining and the sides of the grave were so slippery, that all his efforts to climb out ended in total frustration. When the boy did not return, the mother sent out the older brother to find him. He too cut through the cemetery, and he too failed to see the open grave, and tumbled into the hole. The younger boy was crouching at the other end, and in spite of the darkness and the cold, he found himself beginning to enjoy his older brother's frantic efforts to climb out the slippery walls of the grave. He thought of all the times when his older brother had taken advantage of him and decided he was in a perfect position to even the score. In his eeriest voice, he suddenly shouted from the other side of the grave, "Hey, friend, can't you let a dead man rest in peace?" With that, the older brother who could not climb the six feet out of the hole, literally zoomed out of the grave!

But the power of God is much more than just a shot of adrenalin to the system. It is God's power inside our hearts, power that gives us the courage to witness to others, the power to heal, and the power to minister to those in need in the name of Christ. I like to think of God's power as being like electricity. You cannot see electricity, any more than you can see the wind. But when you put the plug into the socket, you can certainly see what electricity can do. We as Christians are like light cords, and when we let the Spirit of Christ reign supreme in our hearts, it is like being plugged in to the power of God. The whole world can begin to see the light of God's love shining in us because we are in touch with a source of spiritual power greater than anything in this world. Look at what happened to those disciples who heard Jesus tell them they would receive power when the Holy Spirit came upon them. With nothing more than a burning desire to share the good news of Christ's love for sinners, they transformed the whole world with their revolutionary faith. Is it too much to believe that perhaps God wants to transform the broken world in which we live by letting his Spirit empower us in the same way?

3. A Sign Of Guidance

Consider one more truth about the wind. Wind is often a signpost for guidance or direction. The wind sock blowing at an airport tells the pilot in which direction to land his plane. A weatherman can tell what the day will be like tomorrow on the basis of which way the wind is blowing. Jesus compared the Holy Spirit to a counselor, a helper, a friend, a guide through all of life. He promised that his Spirit would continue to stand beside us like a doctor beside his patient, a lawyer beside her client, or a friend beside a person in need.

This is no fair-weather promise of help. It is not like the woman who was flying some years ago across country, when suddenly she noticed that two of the plane's engines were on fire. Panic spread among the passengers as word spread and then suddenly the pilot appeared at the door of the cabin with a large parachute strapped securely to his back. In a cheery voice he said, "Now don't worry about a thing, folks. I'm going for help right away!" God's promise to guide and direct our lives is more than lip service. When you and I come to those moments when the bottom drops out of life, when the blackness of sorrow or tragedy shuts out the light, it is God's Holy Spirit that upholds us, encourages us, and goes with us through the valley of the shadow.

The students at Glasgow University had a custom of jeering those eminent men and women who were appointed by the institution to receive honorary degrees at graduation. When David Livingstone had returned to Scotland after eighteen years in Africa, he was selected to receive an honorary Doctor of Laws degree from Glasgow. His fame preceded him and the students gleefully anticipated the opportunity to jeer at this famous missionary. But when Livingstone appeared on the platform, the students immediately became hushed. The sight of that gaunt and wrinkled figure who had suffered twenty-seven bouts with fever, darkened by the sun, one arm hanging useless by his side as a result of an attack by a lion, awed that assembly. Every ear was listening as Livingstone went to the rostrum to make his remarks. They expected him to speak about his experience in Africa but instead he said, "Shall I tell you what sustained me amidst the toil, the hardships, and the loneliness? It was the most precious of all the promises in the Bible, the words of Jesus who said, 'And lo, I am with you always, even unto the close of the age.' "

Perhaps you wish you had this Spirit of Christ bringing new life, empowering you in your weakness, and directing your life through both joy and sorrow. The promise of Pentecost is you and I can receive that same Spirit by letting Christ reign on the throne of our hearts, and asking God to fill us with his life-giving Spirit. A little lad once asked his grandfather who was a hardy sailor, "Grandpa, what is the wind?" The old man thought for a moment and then said, "I don't know what the wind is, son, but I do know how to hoist a sail." You and I may not fully understand all there is to know about the wind of God, the Holy Spirit. But thank God, we too can hoist a sail. We can open our hearts and receive Jesus Christ as our Lord and Savior, and then ask God to give us this precious gift of his Holy Spirit.

Where Do We Find God?

At the inaugural Assembly of the World Council of Churches in Amsterdam, that great Christian body declared itself to be "a fellowship of Churches which accept Jesus Christ as God and Savior." By the time the World Council held its third Assembly in New Dehli, that basis of union was changed to read, "The World Council of Churches is a fellowship of Churches which confess the Lord Jesus Christ as God and Savior, and *therefore seek to fulfil their common calling to the glory of one God, Father, Son, and Holy Spirit.*"[1] That addition which speaks of God as Father, Son, and Holy Spirit is the direct result of the Eastern Orthodox churches who now represent the largest confessional body in the World Council. The great doctrine of the Eastern Church, the theme of its theology is summed up in the familiar hymn we often sing, "Holy, Holy, Holy, Lord God Almighty . . . God in three Persons, Blessed Trinity." It has always been the insistence of Eastern Christians that we have not said everything we know about God until we have expressed our faith and worshiped him as Father, Son, and Holy Spirit.

Some Christians may say to themselves, "Well, that's nice, but so what? What has all this talk about the Trinity got to do with my life?" However, before we dismiss the Trinity as some mathematical puzzle or academic formula that a few theologians talk about, let me remind you that this belief arose out of the experience of ordinary Christians as a real-life an-

swer to the question, "Where Do We Find God?" That is a
question that is being asked with new urgency by many in our
own time as they listen to the experts telling us there is little
hope for planet earth. If we are not destroyed from without
by nuclear holocaust and a shortage of food, water, and energy,
we will destroy ourselves from within by our greed, our selfishness, and our lust for power. In such a time as ours, men
and women seek with new urgency to find God in their human experience and to know for certain that the God we know
as Father, Son, and Holy Spirit is really in charge.

The uncertainty of our times is well illustrated by a true
story of mistaken identity. A young medical student I once
knew spent his summer vacation working as a butcher in a large
supermarket during the daytime, and worked evenings as an
orderly at the local community hospital. Both jobs, of course,
involved his wearing a white smock. One evening he was in-
structed to wheel a woman patient on a stretcher into surgery.
The patient, already in great fear, looked up at the student,
and let out a scream as she cried, "My God, it's the butcher!"
That's the sense of hopelessness and despair many people feel
in our time, but Christians have always found their hope in
such times by rejoicing in the fact that God has made himself
known to us in three unique ways in our human experience.
Jesus mentions all three of those ways in our Scripture for this
day.

1. God, The Father

Jesus spoke often of God as Father. The word he used is
a familiar word that reminds us of a parent who is above and
beyond us. That parent is older than we are. The very fact that
this parent shared in your creation, brought you into this world,
provided you with a home, cared for you, protected you and
guided you to adulthood, gives that parent a certain natural
supremacy. In that sense we think of God as being above and
beyond us. He is the Creator of the universe, the "lofty One

that inhabits eternity, whose name is Holy."

This was the truth that dawned upon the young Isaiah when he caught a vision of God in the temple, and heard angelic voices singing, "Holy, holy, holy, is the Lord of hosts: the whole earth is full of his glory." Isaiah fell to his knees in penitent despair, crying out, "Woe is me! for I am undone; because I am a man of unclean lips, and I dwell in the midst of a people of unclean lips." The prophet had caught a vision of God's holiness which in the Bible stands for the "only-ness," the "other-ness," the "apart-ness" of the Almighty. For the first time in his life, Isaiah realized the infinite distance separating God from human beings. There burst upon him the truth that in his holiness, God is far removed from human beings in all their failings. He is high above all creation, undisturbed by all the tumultuous conflicts on the earth, and before whom human beings bow in awe, majesty and fear.

Some modern theologians want to get rid of those passages in the Bible that call us to come before the Lord in fear. They say we have enough things to fear in this world without fearing God. But some of those who tremble in fear over the future of the world perhaps do not tremble enough before the Holy God! It is precisely because God is above and beyond us in his power that he is great enough to be our refuge and strength and help in time of need.

Yet in Jesus Christ we discover that this Father God is greater than any human parent in his love and mercy towards his children. Again and again, Jesus encouraged people to come before God the Father as children come to a loving parent who will listen to their cries, who will embrace them as the father of the Prodigal embraced his repentant son, and who will share with them his power and his strength in all of life's troubles. In his Yale Lectures in 1910, Frank Gunsaulus told of a time when Abraham Lincoln, as President of the United States, was sorely troubled with the affairs of state. One day his little son came into the cabinet meeting and said, "I want my father." At this point the Yale Lecturer asks us to imagine that scene.

Tad had been in a fight, and had come off second-best. Covered with blood and dirt, he ran up to Secretary of the Treasury Chase, and cried, "I want my father." But the Secretary looked down and patronizingly and cruelly said, "I will tell the Chief Executive of this nation that you wish to see him." Chase would have spoken the truth, but the boy would still have cried, "I want my father!" Next Tad ran to the Secretary of War. Wiping away the blood and dirt from his eyes, he cried, "I want my father." Secretary of War Stanton heard the boy's appeal and with a grin on his face, said, "I will get for you the Commander in Chief of the Armies of the United States." Stanton knew the President in that capacity. He was telling the truth about Lincoln, but it was not the truth of Lincoln's child. Tad's truth expressed itself in the sob, "I want my father." The great theologians may talk about God as "Ultimate Reality" and "Ground Of All Being," but the truth to which the human heart clings is that we can know God as a Father who is above and beyond us, and a Father who loves us, who cares for us, and helps us in our time of need. Wiping away the blood and dirt from our own souls, we too cry out, "I want my Father!"

2. God The Son

We also celebrate a God who is known to us in our human experience as "The Son." The truth in this designation reminds us of a God who is with us, beside us, around us, and bound up in our life. We call God "Son" because we believe that the Father revealed himself in all his fulness in a moment in time in the life of Jesus of Nazareth. He was God made visible and brought within our experience. In him the mysterious Father above us broke the veil of mystery, came where we are, clothed himself in human flesh, and shared our human life — including suffering and death.

It has always helped me to understand why God became a human being on this earth by reading the story of a father and his young son who were out for a walk on a summer day. As they walked along, the father accidentally stepped on an ant hill. The father and the boy watched the ants scurrying around, some of them dead, others wounded, and the whole ant hill in total confusion. The boy asked, "Dad, what can we do to help those poor ants?" And the father said, "Son, there is really nothing we can do. If you and I could become ants ourselves, we could get down in the dirt with them, and perhaps help them rebuild their home. But you and I are just too big and too far away!'"

What we celebrate on Trinity Sunday is a God who is not too big or too far away to help us in our need. We celebrate the great truth that "God was in Christ, reconciling himself to the world." There were many things that the disciples of our Lord could not understand in their life with him, because they had not yet grasped the enormity of the truth that the Holy One who is above and beyond us has come in Jesus Christ to be with us.

Yet even in pre-Christian times, the writers of the Bible sensed this nearness of God to their everyday lives. The writer of the 90th Psalm could say, "Lord, thou hast been our dwelling-place in all generations." This spiritual genius has an answer to people in our time who fear that as science pushes back the frontiers of knowledge and clears up areas of mystery, that there will be no room left in the scheme of things for God. Such people wonder if God will not be crowded out of the picture altogether. Where can God be in this expanding universe? But the Psalmist saw things the other way around. He believed not that God exists somewhere in the universe but rather that the universe exists within God! In God the worlds consist. He contains all creation. He is our dwelling place in all generations. Paul echoed this same understanding in his sermon to the philosophers in Athens when he spoke of God the Creator, the Lord of heaven and earth, and then added, "Yet he is not far from each one of us, for in him we live and move and have our being." Where do we find God? We find him close at hand, for the God above us is also the God around us, like the very air we breathe, the very atmosphere in which we live and move and have our being, our dwelling place in all generations.

3. The Holy Spirit

We have spoken of a God who is above and beyond us, and a God who is beside us and around us. However, there is a third dimension of God in human experience, the experience of a God who dwells deep within us. When someone tries to describe the triune God, I often think of that harassed wife and mother who found herself living in a three-generation household where the grandfather, the father, and the son all answered to the same first name. One day the phone rang and the poor woman heard a voice asking to speak to Jim. Her family could not help overhearing her say in obvious despair, "Which one do you want: Jim the father, Jim the son, or Jim the holy terror?"

The Spirit we speak of is not some holy terror, but the Spirit of Jesus Christ that we believe dwells deep in the human heart. Even nonreligious people will talk about spirit as distinct from body. They talk all the time about the spirit of love or hatred or joy or fear or hope that fills the human heart. However, when Christians talk about God as Holy Spirit, we believe that a more than human spirit, the Spirit of God revealed in his Son Jesus Christ, can dwell within the temple of our bodies. That was exactly what happened to the disciples on Pentecost and it has been the experience of Christians all down the ages — that when they opened their hearts in faith and yielded their lives in obedience to Christ, the Spirit of Christ took possession of them and filled them with grace and power. This is a God who is as present now as he was when he walked this earth as Jesus of Nazareth.

Some years ago a group of Russian peasants met for worship in secret. They knew full well that if discovered by the authorities, they would probably receive the death penalty for breaking the law. While their worship was proceeding, the door was suddenly thrown open and the secret police entered. "Take these people's names," commanded the officer in charge. The names were written down — a total of thirty men and women. The officers lined up the captives and prepared to take them away when suddenly an old man in the group said there was one name missing from the list of those present. "Who is it?" demanded the officer. "Speak up, old man, or I will have you shot right now." With a remarkably strong voice, the old man said, "The Lord Jesus Christ is here with us as well." "Ah!" said the Russian officer. "That does not matter! Take them away!"

But it does matter! For Christians believe that through the Holy Spirit Jesus is present every time we gather in his name. He is the one who takes this Gospel out of history and out of the realms of eternity, and plants it right in your heart and in mine. This is the Holy Spirit, God with us now in all his power to convict us of our sin, and to convince us of his righteousness and mercy. This is the same God from whom we can never escape.

The ancient writer of the 139th Psalm, though he lived in pre-Christian times, had come to this all consuming conviction about God: Though we lose our hold upon him, he never loses his hold upon us. Though we turn our backs upon him, he does not go away. Though we run from him, yet he follows us. Though we try to hide from him, yet he tracks us down. "Whither shall I go from thy Spirit? or whither shall I flee from thy presence? If I ascend up into heaven, thou art there; If I make my bed in hell, behold, thou art there."

This is not a God who is some sort of celestial Big Brother, or even some ghostly Hound of Heaven who pursues us to the farthest limits of space. This is the indwelling Spirit of God, the very depth of our being to which as Christians we are indissolubly bound. We cannot escape from this Spirit any more than we can escape from ourselves. Where do we find God?

The answer is, we do not find him, but rather it is he who finds us. It is always he who takes the initiative and reaches into our lives with irresistible grace and power. The Father above us, who has revealed his love in the Son beside us, has shed abroad his love in our hearts by the presence of the Holy Spirit within us. This is the God who loves us with an everlasting love, and his love will never let us go. All praise be to him, Father, Son, and Holy Spirit!

Making a Lot Out of a Little

A man came home from work, kissed his wife, and asked, "What's for dinner?" She replied, "Charles Steak." "What in the world is *that*?" asked the tired husband. "Well," said the wife, "at today's prices, to call it 'chuck steak' seems a bit undignified!" The price of food today is startling. Just ask anyone who has been to the grocery store lately! Yet, how would you feel if you suddenly were responsible, on a limited budget, for feeding more than 5,000 people? That's the problem that confronted Jesus' disciples one day when a huge crowd had spent the entire day at a picnic spot beside the Sea of Galilee. All day long this crowd had hung on Jesus' every word, but now they were tired, hungry, and exhausted. Some had come by boat to this side of the lake, but many others faced a long, weary walk back to their homes. The nearest town was a crossroads called Magdala which was about a mile and a half away. That may not sound like a great distance to us, but do not forget that this crowd had no Chevrolets, Fords, or Volkswagens sitting in the parking lot. Nor were there any convenient McDonalds or Burger Kings on the street corners in Magdala! Where could the disciples get enough food to feed this crowd? And worse yet, where could they get the money to pay for it? In the account of this story given in John's Gospel, the disciples apparently figured that it would take more than a half a year's wages to feed this mob.

It is not surprising to find the disciples of Jesus saying to him, "Send this crowd away. It's getting late. There's nothing we can do for them. We're preachers, not hotel and restaurant keepers!" But Jesus will not let them do it. His question is, "What do you have on hand?" It is then that the disciples bring forward a little boy with five loaves and two fish. Those loaves were probably no bigger than a softball and the fish no larger than sardines. That's not much food for more than 5,000 hungry souls! Yet, when Jesus blessed those tiny loaves and fish, all were fed and satisfied. Of all the miracles Jesus ever performed in his ministry, this is the one story that has come down to us in each of the four Gospels. No one in the early Church ever forgot the day when Jesus made a lot out of a little!

Ever since that day, theologians have tried to offer suggestions for what really took place. One group insists that this was in reality a sort of sacramental meal. That is, the people were spiritually nourished by the morsel of food they received, much as people feel refreshed by the bread and wine of Holy Communion. In actuality, according to those theologians, the people only received a crumb of food, but that food brought strength to their souls, and they went away satisfied.

Still another group of theologians have explained that the real miracle in the feeding of the 5,000 was how a little boy's generosity turned a stingy crowd into a group of men and women willing to share what they had. These interpreters argue that no one in his or her right mind would have gone out to such a lonely place without taking along a picnic lunch. The problem was that there were others who had tagged along who had brought no food, and those with the provisions were afraid they would get none if all had to share in common. They did not like the idea of a covered dish supper — until they were shamed into sharing what they had by one unselfish little boy who gave all he had.

And still other theologians insist that the feeding of the 5,000 is like a re-enactment of God's feeding his people in the wilderness with the manna from heaven. For them, this is simply a miracle of multiplication, and if for God all things are possible, why not the feeding of more than 5,000 men, women, and children?

All three of these traditional interpretations only scratch the surface of the meaning in this story for our lives. This is not simply a story of how Jesus fed five thousand people on a hillside overlooking the Sea of Galilee centuries ago. This is the story of how Jesus Christ, through the power of the Holy Spirit can still make a lot out of a little in your life and in mine. It is a story of how Christ can still satisfy the deepest longings and hungers not only in our bodies but in our souls. Let us look together at four of the ingredients that were essential on that day when God made a lot out of a little.

1. Thanksgiving To God

Luke records for us that Jesus took the loaves and the fish and, looking to heaven, he gave thanks before distributing them to the crowd. The blessing he may have used was the one familiar to every Jewish household: "Blessed art Thou, O Lord God, King of the Universe, who bringest forth bread from the earth." Essential to an understanding of this miracle is the fact that it began with thanksgiving and praise to God.

Perhaps you are saying to yourself, "We say grace before every meal in our house . . . and it hasn't helped a bit in filling up those teenage boys of ours!" Or perhaps you recall the two little boys who were discussing whether to say grace before a meal. One asked, "Do you say a prayer of thanks before you eat in your family?" "Heck, no!" said the other boy. "My mom's a good cook!" We smile, but the truth is that we are not a very thankful people. We may mumble a few words before dinner, and give our annual nod to God each November at Thanksgiving, but how many of us actually begin our days by praising God and thanking him for all we have? There was an old Scottish minister who always began his Sunday service with the words, "We praise Thee, O God." One

Sunday it was pouring rain. The wind was howling, and many worshipers had stayed at home. One church member turned to another sitting beside her and said, "I wonder what our minister will find to praise God about this morning?" At the appointed hour the pastor entered the pulpit and said, "We praise Thee, O God, especially that every Sunday morning is not like this one!"

It is easy to be thankful and to praise God when all is going well in our lives, when the skies are clear, the birds are singing, and all our needs are met. But out there on a hillside with five or six thousand hungry people and no money, it is absolutely astounding that the first thing Jesus did was to give thanks. That says to me that the first ingredient in asking God to make a lot out of a little is a thankful heart — an awareness that we are dependant upon God for everything we have and everything we are. Our national day of Thanksgiving had its origin in that time when our Pilgrim forebearers found themselves in the midst of poverty and illness. But instead of endless prayers to God for deliverance, they set aside a day of thanksgiving to God for their freedom and for what little they possessed. If historians are correct, food was so scarce at that first Thanksgiving meal with the Indians, that corn had to be rationed five kernals to a person. But out of that desperate poverty, God made a lot out of a little, and it all began when people gave thanks to God.

2. Willingness To Share

The second ingredient that must be present when God makes a lot out of a little is the willingness to share. The real hero of this story is the little boy who was willing to do something radical and generous to meet the need of that crowd. In fact, he gave everything he had. I well remember when my wife and I were privileged to visit Israel. We stopped one afternoon in what is now called the Church Of The Multiplication. It was built in the third century, on the spot where Jesus fed the 5,000, and on its walls is a mosaic that depicts the scene of this miracle. What do you think that early artist recorded as the most significant event in this story? Was it the abundance of food? Was it the frantic disciples, or the hungry crowd? No, the central feature in that mosaic is the boy handing over his five loaves and his two fish to Jesus. The message of those walls was, if we will share *everything* we have with Jesus Christ, there will always be more than enough to go around. What a contrast there is between that generous little boy, and many of us who spend most of our lives worrying over whether we will have enough resources to see us through! Many of us, especially as we get older, hold on tighter and tighter to our possessions, to our money, and to our good health, in the fear that we may not have enough. Yet here is a mere boy who lets Jesus Christ have everything, and when he does, God is able to make a lot out of a little.

History is full of examples of how God has made a lot out of a little when people have dared to share all they have for the advancement of his Kingdom. An old Negro lady came to Booker T. Washington. She was hobbling on her cane. He was raising funds for the founding of Tuskegee Institute. She was clad in rags and obviously was a person of very little means, but she said, "Mr. Washington, God knows that I have spent the best years of my life in slavery, and God knows that I am ignorant and poor and have very little money. But I know you are trying to make better men and women for the colored race, and I want you to take these six eggs I have been saving up, and use them to help those boys and girls get an education." Booker T. Washington said that no other gift he received touched him so deeply as the gift of those six eggs.[1] The story of that woman's willingness to share all she had to help others touched the hearts of hundreds of others whose donations made Tuskegee Institute a reality. Once again, one person's willingness to share helped God to make a lot out of a little.

3. Human Hands Essential

Notice a third ingredient in this story of how God makes a lot out of a little: God always does that through human hands. It is ordinary people using their gifts for the glory of God that produces such amazing results. No doubt the people who ate that day on the hillside by the Sea of Galilee were able to do so more freely, because the food came directly from the hands of Jesus' disciples. Had the food fallen from heaven by some sort of magic, they would probably have been too terrified to eat!

God always works through human hands, and sometimes we miss the miracles he performs in our lives, because we fail to appreciate what the Spirit can do with the gifts God has given. I find myself as a pastor visiting the hospitals, more and more led to pray prayers of thanksgiving to God for the miracles of healing that come through the hands of doctors and nurses. Many times they are the vehicles through which God makes a lot out of a little in our society. But each one of us has some sort of gift that God can multiply in his service. We must never think that the only work Jesus has today is preaching, teaching, and praying in public. The disciples in this story remind us that God can use the most ordinary person in meeting the deep hungers of both the body and the spirit of people today.

William Barclay tells the story of a young preacher who was poor and had a hard struggle to get his education. Throughout those years he was given constant encouragement by an old shoemaker in that town. When the young man graduated and was ordained, the old shoemaker said to him: "Will you do me a great favor? Will you let me make your shoes for nothing?" The old shoemaker then explained that he had always hoped to become a preacher himself, but things had never worked out. He said to the young man, "I want to make your shoes, so that when you preach, I will think of you standing in those shoes, preaching the gospel in the way I never got the chance to do.''[2] That old shoemaker was serving God not only in using his gift to make shoes, but in allowing another to multiply his efforts to bring the Gospel of Jesus Christ to hungry hearts.

Back in the summer of 1979 I was privileged to attend a conference of 5,000 church women on the campus of Purdue University. One of the principal speakers was a woman lawyer from Korea. She told us of the resentment and hatred she met in her own land when, as a woman, she began to use her skills to defend the rights of poor people in her country. Eventually she was imprisoned for her outspoken faith and her attempt to change government policy in dealing with the poor. She told us of how at first she was terribly discouraged and felt her life had been a waste. But then she said, "When my right to practice law was taken away, God moved in the hearts of 160 other lawyers in my country to volunteer their time to help my clients!" What amazing things happen when this God, who makes a lot out of a little, moves our human hands and hearts in such a way that one lawyer is multiplied by one hundred and sixty!

4. Jesus Is The Bread Of Life

Thanksgiving, the willingness to share, and the essential use of human hands — these are all ingredients that must be present when God makes a lot out of a little. But there is one key ingredient that goes to the heart of why Christians have never forgotten that day long ago when Jesus fed more than 5,000 people. That key is that Jesus is the Bread Of Life. This is no simple story from the long ago and far away of how Jesus once filled people's empty stomachs. This is a story of how the Living Christ can still satisfy the deepest longings, and the deepest hunger in our hearts and souls.

One of the besetting difficulties of our age is that often, we do not even realize how lost we have become. There was once a little boy who got lost in a huge shopping mall. His

parents were looking frantically for him, but in the meantime,
the security guards had located the boy and taken him to their
office. The parents were paged over the public address system and rushed to the security office. There was their little
boy, sitting on a bench, happily eating an ice cream cone. But
when he saw his parents, he suddenly burst into tears. One
of the security guards said to the parents, "How about that!
That little fellow didn't even know he was lost until he was
found!" My guess is that the little boy has a lot of company.
We seem to have become a generation of people who are un-
happy — who complain of boredom, or despair, or just plain
emptiness deep within our spirits.

Many persons have tried to satisfy that longing by seeking
to fulfill every possible human appetite, but no amount of power or prestige or possessions ever seems to satisfy that hunger
within our souls. Others of us have tried to fill that void with
an ethical and moral life that has brought us much praise from
those around us, but like the Pharisees in Jesus' day, it has
left us with the question asked by the Rich Young Ruler, "What
more must I do to inherit eternal life?" In a novel published
many years ago entitled, *If Winter Comes*, the author has the
hero say, "We are all plugging along like mad, because we
are all looking for something. You can read it in half the faces
you see; some wanting and knowing that they are wanting
something; others wanting something but putting up with it,
content to be discontent. What is it that we are all looking for,
that universal something that is wanting?"[3]

What we are looking for is not some*thing*, but rather, some-
one. Augustine said it long ago: "Our hearts are restless until
they find their rest in Thee." That which we seek is the Bread
of Life. It is Jesus who brings us that bread. It is Jesus who
came into this world to make life worth living. He takes our
lives which seem to us to be so daily, and with his power and
his presence and his purpose, he makes them into lives that
are full and rich and significant.

The old Welsh hymn that we sing in many of our churches

is the heartfelt prayer of those who look to God to make a
lot out of a little:

> *Guide me, O Thou great Jehovah, Pilgrim through this barren land;*
> *I am weak, but Thou art mighty; Hold me with Thy powerful hand;*
> *Bread of heaven, Bread of heaven, Feed me till I want no more.*

Luke 7:1-10

Proper 4 (Common)
Pentecost 2 (Lutheran)
Ordinary Time 9 (Roman Catholic)

The Outsider

I have always admired this Roman centurion who came seeking the help of our Lord. Unlike so many of these career officers who commanded military garrisons in the occupied countries, coarse and brutal soldiers, here was a man who was refined, sensitive, and humane. Whether attracted to Jewish religious faith or not, he could still see the value of supporting that faith instead of ridiculing it. He had even provided the funds for the building of a new synagogue. Now he was before Jesus seeking the healing his sick servant needed so desparately. Even that act marks this centurion as a person of unusual sensitivity. In the ancient world a slave was valued no higher than a piece of real estate! This soldier's affectionate concern, the humility of his approach to Jesus, and his spiritual discernment were clearly greater than that of many of the professedly religious people our Lord encountered. As Jesus marveled at the simplicity of this man's faith, he said to the multitude, "I tell you that not even in Israel have I found such faith."

There is something familiar about this Roman centurion. He is typical of many people who, while professing no allegiance to the community of faith, still display a remarkable degree of genuine faith. Here is Mr. White. His wife comes to church almost every Sunday, but he himself rarely attends. Yet most of us know him to be a fine person, generous and

unselfish, a good husband and father. Often he has purchased
something needed at the church and forgotten to send a bill.
He seems to be a person who, as someone has put it, spends
his breath arguing that there is no God, and yet spends his
life proving that there is. Yet, for all the Christlikeness in his
life, Mr. White is an outsider when it comes to the church.

Here is Mrs. Black. She reads her Bible daily and probably knows it better than most preachers! She gives evidence
of a warm and personal faith in God, and yet she too stands
outside the church. Her problem is the awesome gap between
what is professed so loudly on Sundays, and what is demonstrated in everyday life from Monday through Saturday. She,
too, is an outsider. And then there is Miss Smith. Unlike the
others, Miss Smith comes to worship, but she has never felt
that she could actually become a member of the church. You
see, she has so many questions about Christ, about the Creation of the world, and about the Scriptures, that she feels un-
worthy of becoming a member. She believes in God, but she
still has many questions to be answered. She's really uncom-
fortable in the presence of those Christians who seem to have
all the answers, so she too remains an outsider. Wherever we
go, we meet these modern counterparts of the Roman centurion
— people we admire and respect, but who stand outside the
church.

Not all religious people are inside the church. The Bible
itself does not pretend that the church has a monopoly on
religion. Instead, the Bible talks about the sovereignty of God,
and that means that God does not stand idly around shifting
from one foot to the other, waiting to be recognized or received
before he can do something with a human life. God in Christ
is the Lord of all life and the source of all good, no matter
what name it uses or where it is found. Within the church today we deplore the secularism which has penetrated all areas
of our culture as a worm penetrates a delicious apple on a tree.
Where are the religious themes that once dominated the art,
the music, the literature of two centuries ago? Once human

beings built their universities, painted their pictures, and composed their symphonies to the glory of God; now they seem only to glorify themselves. Does that mean that we can write off modern culture as irreligious? The painful truth we must consider is that, far from being devoid of religion, all those areas of life which we commonly denote as secular may come closer to the heart of true spirituality than we ever imagined.

Diogenes Allen of Princeton Theological Seminary has written a book entitled, *The Three Outsiders.* He uses the writings of Blaise Pascal, Soren Kierkegaard and Simone Weil to illustrate how three persons, who stood outside the institutional church in their respective eras, may well have been asking the most profound and disturbing questions about what it means to be a Christian in the contemporary world. George Gallup, Jr., in his recent book, *Who Do Americans Say That I Am?* comes to the conclusion as a result of his surveys of public opinion that many Americans are not being served adequately by their churches. But, he says, their interest in spiritual values has increased, and their essential trust in Jesus Christ, like that of this Roman centurion, is greater than that of many church members. What is the effect of these outsiders upon those of us who sit in the church pews or stand in its pulpits week by week?

1. They Judge Us

These persons outside the institutional church always bring into bold relief the paltriness of our Christianity, and compel us to ask ourselves, "What do you do more than others?" Look at the deep sense of reverence we see in this centurion. Too often in our own time the Church has become so humanistic in its worship and so secular in its outlook that it has lost the dimension of the supernatural in its life. It is a strange thing to say, but this most essential element in true spirituality appears more often in the scientific laboratory than in the church of our time. The late Albert Einstein was not a practicing Jew.

He belonged to no orthodox religious community, yet Einstein called himself a religious man. Listen to his own words: "The most beautiful thing we can experience is the mysterious. It is the source of all true art and science. He to whom this emotion is a stranger, who can no longer pause to wonder and stand in awe, is as good as dead; his eyes are closed. This insight into the mystery of life, coupled though it be with fear, has given rise to religion. To know that what is impenetrable to us really exists, manifesting itself as the highest wisdom and the most radiant beauty which our dull facilities can comprehend only in their most primitive forms — this knowledge, this feeling is at the center of true religiousness. In this sense, and in this sense only, I belong to the ranks of devoutly religious men."[1]

Those outside the church, like Einstein and this faithful centurion, stand in judgment over us. They challenge the gap they so clearly see between our believing and our behaving. They are waiting to be convinced, but they can see no reason for belonging to the church, because there seems so little difference in the lives of church members from those outside the church. A little boy said to his father, "Dad, did you always go to church when you were a little boy?" The father, in pious tones, said, "Son, when I was a boy like you, I never missed a Sunday." The little boy turned to his mother and said, "You see, Mom, that's what I mean. It won't do me any good either!"

I see in this centurion one who quite honestly puts us to shame, for he possesses the reverence, the humility, and the faith that many of us talk about but fail to exhibit in our everyday lives. Mahatma Gandhi was not far from the Kingdom of God. In many ways he was one of those fine persons outside the church who lived a more discerning spiritual life than many within. Gandhi was profoundly affected by the teachings of Jesus, and in his early life, he almost became a Christian. He told of his contact with a Christian family in South Africa, people who gave him a standing invitation to dinner every Sunday and afterward took him to their church. The service, apparently, did not make a favorable impression on young Gandhi. He found the sermons uninspiring, and the congregation so worldly-minded that he concluded they were in church only to impress their neighbors. He confessed that he had a hard time keeping awake, and would have felt ashamed except that some of his white-skinned neighbors suffered the same difficulty. He said, "I cannot go on like this," and he gave up attending the service.[2] Like this Roman centurion, those outside the church often stand in judgment over us.

2. They Inspire Us

But we do these folks outside the Church an injustice if they only embarrass us with their faith. More often they become our greatest incentive to holier and Christlike living. In the Christian life, we must not compare ourselves with broken-down, blasphemous wrecks of humanity, but rather, with the very best that the world outside the church can produce. These are the persons who must become our norm. These we must surpass. These are the people, like this ancient Roman, who inspire us.

Too often we meet people who talk in biblical terms, but whose lives lack the depth of social and moral responsibility that we see in those outside the institutional church. A seminary student once said, "I have a biblical outlook on life. I'm going to raise Cain as long as I am Abel." But it is sobering to realize how many of the great humanitarians, the social reformers and public servants have worked independently of organized Christianity. Sir William Osler is another of those profoundly religious persons who stood outside the church. One biographer describes him walking down the main street of Montreal on a bitterly cold winter morning and taking off his overcoat and putting it on the back of a starving beggar. That typified the young man who later became Regius Professor of Medicine at Oxford and drew from more than one of his friends a comment like this: "My intimate associations with him as a guide, philosopher, and friend lead me to the belief that he was of all men the most Christlike in his life and the most God-like in his attitudes." The biographer concludes the Montreal incident by saying, "It is singular how all who were thrown with Dr. Osler felt his likeness to Christ. Always before them they saw the Divine Physician. They could not see the one without thinking of the other."[3]

3. They Challenge Us

But most importantly of all, these persons of faith outside the church of Jesus Christ challenge us and the validity of our own Christian experience. We have always taken it for granted that Christianity should be a witnessing religion. We are bound by our Lord's commission to share our faith and to bring all people into the household of faith. Are we then going to make exceptions? Are we going to assume that, because a person has achieved so much apart from organized religion, they therefore have no need of our Gospel and can get along without the church's message and fellowship? If so, we reduce Christianity to what many of its critics would like to make it — a pink pill for personality problems, a crutch for weaklings, and a refuge for the inadequate. These folks outside the church challenge us to discover that even the finest human beings we know still need God, for without God their lives can never be complete and can never achieve their highest potential.

Sometimes talking to these men and women outside the church about a Savior is a bit like throwing a life preserver to a person sitting safely and comfortably on the seashore. They don't respond to the old arguments, nor to the notion that all human beings are nothing but worthless sinners. But they are still creatures with a soul and therefore with hungers and longings that only God can satisfy. The great truth about the Roman centurion was this: Christ could do something for him. Despite all his strength, all his innate goodness, he still reached a point of helplessness, a situation beyond his own ability to manage. He needed Christ, and in faith he turned to Christ for something he did not have within himself.

Charles Colson, the Watergate conspirator who spent a year in prison, wrote a book called *Born Again*. He tells how he overcame his pride and turned to Christ for help. He had been the fair-haired boy of the White House, Special Counsel to the President, Nixon's hatchet man. There was nothing he could not do. Then suddenly everything fell apart. He found he could not handle his life any more. He went to see a friend, Tom Phillips, who talked to him about his soul and read from a book by C. S. Lewis. Lewis spoke of pride as a spiritual career, the complete anti-God state of mind. Then Phillips prayed with him. "Lord," he said, "we pray for Chuck and his family, that you might open his heart and show him the light and the way." God answered that prayer marvellously and mightily. He brought Charles Colson to the point of saying, "Lord Jesus, I believe you. I accept you. Please come into my life. I commit it to you."[4] Even the strongest, most self-reliant and dedicated human being outside the fellowship of Christ needs something that only Christ can give. And when we come in humility, asking for Christ's help, we can be sure it will be given to us.

The outsiders judge us. They inspire us, and they challenge us. Let us never forget this Roman centurion, of whom our Lord said, "I tell you, not even in Israel have I found such faith."

Luke 7:11-17

Proper 5 (Common)
Pentecost 3 (Lutheran)
Ordinary Time 10 (Roman Catholic)

Making People Whole

In a tender and moving biography, James Davidson Ross tells about the migraine headaches with which is beloved wife, Clare, suffered for many years of her life. The attacks would come every two or three weeks, and were of such an intensity, she could not get out of bed for twenty-four hours at a time. The pain was so terrible that Clare's vision was out of focus and her speech was distorted. Doctors offered no hope of a cure. The only thing to be done was to get her to bed, darken the room, and leave her alone to suffer in agony. After a particularly rough attack, Ross decided to take his wife to a healing service sponsored by the Order of St. Luke in a nearby church. The pastor leading the service prayed for Clare and called upon others present to come forward and to lay their hands upon her. Miraculously, Clare left that service feeling better than she had felt for many years, and to the end of her life, she never again suffered a migraine attack. Her husband writes: "The cynics may say that a psychosomatic complaint had been dealt with by psychological means. In fact, the cynics may say anything they want! But in faith Clare had taken twenty years of sickness to God, and in faith she had left that sickness with him, believing that God alone had the power to make her whole."[1]

Accounts of miraculous healings always raise many questions, and the story of Jesus' healing of the widow's son at

Nain is no exception. Our immediate response is often one of skepticism, much like the mother of a little boy who asked her son what he had learned in Sunday church school that day. "We heard all about a man named Moses. He went behind the lines and rescued the Israelites. Then he came to the Red Sea, and called in his engineers to build a pontoon bridge. After the Israelites got across, he saw the Egyptian tanks approaching, so he got on his walkie-talkie and called in the Air Force who sent dive bombers and blew up the bridge with all the Egyptians still on it." "Now, son," said the Mother. "Is that really what your teacher told you?" "Well, not exactly, but if I told you what she told us, you'd never believe it in a thousand years!" Such is often our response when we hear of miraculous happenings.

In the situation described by Luke, the young man is already dead. His funeral is in progress! But with our modern scientific minds, we recall the fact that, in the hot climate of ancient Palestine, persons were buried with astonishing quickness, and given the rudimentary medical knowledge of the times, some were pronounced dead who really were in a coma or trance. However, the consistent witness of the Bible is that our Lord healed many persons and restored them to a wholeness of body, mind, and spirit they did not possess before they met Jesus Christ. Until quite recently, many Christians have ignored this healing ministry of Jesus, or considered it the sole property of Mary Baker Eddy and her followers in Christian Science. However, a closer study of the Gospels has revealed that Jesus spent as much time in healing in his earthly ministry as he did in preaching and teaching. In every case the healing that Christ brought to people was not the sensational performing of a miracle for its own sake, but rather the compassionate use of the powers he possessed to defeat disease, death, and sin. An indication of just how important this healing ministry was to Jesus is given to us in that account of John the Baptizer, sitting alone in prison, wondering if Jesus really is the promised Messiah. He sends messengers to Jesus, asking, "Are you he who is to come, or shall we look for another?'' To which Jesus replies: "Go and tell John what you have seen and heard: the blind receive their sight, the lame walk, the lepers are cleansed, the deaf hear, and the poor have good news preached to them." With this story of the healing of the widow's son as our focus, let us explore together the way in which our Lord used the healing power of God to make people whole.

1. Who Was Healed?

Let's begin with the persons who were the object of Jesus' healing ministry. They seem to fall into two categories. The first group are those who suffered from some organic physical illness. These would include blind persons like Bartimaeus, the epileptic boy with his father at the foot of the Mount of Transfiguration, and the Ten Lepers who were cleansed. William Barclay notes that there are three stories in the Gospels which tell of how Jesus raised the daughter of Jairus from her deathbed, he raised the son of the widow at Nain from his funeral casket, and he raised Lazarus from the tomb itself. Barclay concludes: "We cannot tell whether or not this progression is deliberate; but it does show us this — that there is nothing too difficult for Jesus to do."[2]

But it is precisely at this point that many people, especially those in the medical profession, feel that the Christian church has no business interfering in the case of those who are physically ill. These persons insist that organic physical illness demands the expertise of scientific medical knowledge and the practitioners of religion ought to keep their hands off. Sadly, many Christians within the church have forgotten that all healing comes from God, whether through the hands of a skilled physician or as a direct answer to prayer. Many have seen prayers for healing as a kind of last-resort measure when all else has failed. Only last year I was visiting an elderly lady in the hospital. Her doctor was just leaving, and he said to me, "Well Reverend, there's nothing more I can do for her;

it's up to you and the undertaker now!''

Too often Christians have faced physical illness like the old man who was out in a rowboat when a great storm came up. His little boat kept filling with water. His oars were washed away. His bailing bucket was gone, In desperation he lifted up his eyes to heaven and said, "Lord, I haven't bothered you for twenty years; get me out of this mess, and I won't bother you for twenty more!" Yet, in the face of this unwillingness on the part of the modern church to link faith to the healing of physical illness, the Bible steadfastly proclaims that the power of God brought wholeness, not only to those Christ touched directly, but to those who experienced the power of God in the radiant lives of his early followers.

The other group who were the object of Jesus' healing ministry were those who had illnesses related to mental, emotional, and spiritual problems in their lives. Jesus brought wholeness to lives like those of the Gadarene demoniac who was tortured by mental illness. He brought a wholeness of purpose to people like Zachaeus and Mary of Magdala, people whose lives had become fragmented by sin. Always his concern for people went beyond the merely physical symptoms to the root causes of their illness. An amusing story is told by Dr. Norman Vincent Peale, from his own ministry. Dr. Peale had preached a sermon in a church in New Jersy. Afterwards, a woman came up to him and said, "Dr. Peale, I listened to your sermon but I want to tell you that I itch all over!" Peale replied that he had experienced many reactions to his preaching over the years, but never had anyone said that his message made them itch all over. The woman insisted that her discomfort was particularly acute after she had attended worship. Curious, Peale contacted the woman's doctor. He confirmed that his patient did indeed have an itchy rash on her body and was running a low temperature. But after exhaustive testing, he could find no physical cause for her suffering. The doctor, however, did tell Dr. Peale that his patient had had a serious falling out with her sister twenty years before over the settling of their father's estate. He could not be sure, but his best medical guess was that this woman was consumed by her hatred of her sister. Dr. Peale called the woman into his office and told her that he was convinced her itching was caused not by some physical malady but by the hatred deeply rooted in her soul. "There is only one physician who can help you," he said, "and that is the Great Physician, Jesus Christ." At first the woman furiously denied the problem, but then the flood gates opened and she poured out her twenty years of bitterness and disappointment. Dr. Peale prayed with her, and then the woman prayed for her sister, and for the healing of their relationship. From that moment, the itchiness never recurred.[3]

2. Why Did Jesus Heal?

Dr. Peale's modern story leads us, however, to the deeper question of why Jesus was so concerned about sick persons. What was the motivation behind his healing ministry? When you study the healing miracles of Jesus, there is a word that literally leaps off the page at you. It is the word "whole," meaning complete. Jesus asked the man at the Pool of Bethesda, "Wilt thou be made *whole*?" To blind Bartimaeus he explains, "Your faith has made you *whole*. It is that desire to see hurting men and women made whole that takes us to the heart of Jesus' healing ministry. When Jesus saw that sorrowing widow at Nain, he was moved with compassion for her. The Greek word which we translate as "compassion" literally means to be moved to the depths of one's being. It is a word used repeatedly in the Gospels of Jesus. When he saw the multitudes with all their sick people, he was moved with compassion. When he saw hungry people, far from home, he was moved with compassion. Jesus could not see anyone in trouble or pain, or hunger or sorrow without being moved with compassion, and his compassion moved him to action.

The love in the heart of Jesus for that poor woman whose

son had died prompted him to take an incredible risk on her behalf. Luke tells us that Jesus touched the bier in which the young man lay. To us that means nothing special, but to an ancient Jew, the touching of a dead body meant that a person was unclean for at least seven days. Jesus took a risk to be of help, but his compassion and his desire to use the power of God to make people whole overcame any reservations he may have had. Down through the centuries people with that same compassion in their hearts for hurting persons have gladly taken such risks. A young man named James Phipps put his own life in jeopardy to assist Edward Jenner in 1796 in developing a vaccination for small-pox. Sir James Simpson in 1847 tested ether as a simple anaesthetic on himself before sharing his discovery with the world.

Even in our own time, the people of Christ continue to risk their own lives as they are moved by compassion to minister in Jesus' name to those who are sick. The Episcopal Church of the Good Shepherd in Hartford, Connecticut, is now trying to pick up where medical science leaves off in the care of AIDS victims. The Rev. Thaddeus Bennett is now conducting a monthly healing service to give support and comfort to AIDS sufferers and others whose lives have been affected by the disease. Asked if offering a healing service might not give participants false hopes that they will be cured, Bennett explained that to "heal" and to "cure" are not synonymous. "We don't mean that if you have AIDS or any other diseases that you'll be cured by coming to our service, but if you look at the stories of Jesus, you will see there is something powerful about people gathering together in the presence of God; the potential is there for something to happen."[4] Pastor Bennett went on to explain that healing can occur on many different levels. There is physical, mental and spiritual healing, and when you look at the human condition in a holistic sense, there is a real place for Christ's people in the healing process on all levels. That same compassion for hurting people that moved our Lord still moves others in his name to be a part of such a healing ministry.

4. How Did Christ Heal?

But our skeptical minds ask not only *who* was healed, and *why* did Jesus heal; we want to know *how* did Christ heal? I would not for even a moment pretend that I could explain how Jesus Christ performed the miracles he did. The one thread that seems to flow through so many of these accounts of healing, however, is this: When Jesus' help was sought in *faith*, the power of God flowed through Jesus to heal, to restore, and in this case, to resurrect a man from the dead. Here we confront a genuine mystery. Both in biblical times and in our own, there are definite limitations on our knowledge of illness and what makes people get well. What Jesus demonstrated in his life is that there are no limits at all on the love and power of Almighty God. For God, all things are possible, even those which our finite minds can never explain.

The truth of God's power at work in our lives was beautifully illustrated in the life of a dedicated Christian doctor who is a close, personal friend of mine. He is a neurosurgeon and some years ago one of his patients was a parishioner of mine whom we shall call Mr. Jones. Mr. Jones had a tumor on his spine that was cancerous. My friend operated to remove the tumor, but shortly after the surgery, he came to the patient's room to break the sad news that the malignancy was more widespread than he had originally thought. Mr. Jones listened and then asked, "Doctor, how long have I got?" My doctor friend told him that most people with the same diagnosis lived about six months. A long silence followed, and then it was the doctor who broke the quietness by asking, "Would you like me to pray with you?" The doctor opened his medical bag, got out a well-worn copy of Luke's Gospel, and together the physician and the patient read God's Word and prayed together. They did not pray for a miracle, but instead asked for the power of God to be at work in both of their lives. A few days later, the doctor discharged his patient from the hospital. Four months later Mr. Jones went back to work, and in the last eleven years, he has not missed a single day of work because of illness. Twice a year he goes to the University of Pennsylvania Hospital in Philadelphia to check to see if the cancer is spreading. For eleven years there has been no sign of further illness.

My doctor friend does not pray with all his patients, but deep in his heart is the conviction that all healing is from God, that his medical skill is but one facet of a much larger healing process in which God uses his power to make people whole. Not every patient who goes to my friend as a physician is miraculously cured, but I have never met a single patient of his who was not strengthened and helped by this gentle person in whom the Spirit of Jesus Christ dwells in such power.

All praise be given to the God in whose limitless power we can be made whole!

Luke 7:36—8:3 [C, RC]   *Proper 6 (Common)*
Luke 7:36-50 [L]   *Pentecost 4 (Lutheran)*
Ordinary Time 11 (Roman Catholic)

By The Hair of a Sinner

Some years ago, I remember reading a book whose title I cannot recall, in which the writer speculated that Jesus of Nazareth was married. But even the author of that book had to admit that there is not one word, not one intimation, not one shred of suggestion in the Bible that Jesus ever got married.

Nonetheless, Jesus had many followers and close friends who were women of his own age. The respect and kindness, the love and concern with which he treated them has become a turning point in human history. It was Jesus Christ who helped women emerge from being chattels of men to being human souls with every right of personhood. Take for instance this story about a woman who in desperation, washes Jesus' feet with her tears.

While there is no record of Jesus ever playing tennis or skiing, the Bible does mention one thing we like to do which he also liked — and that's attending dinner parties. There are several occasions in the Gospels where Jesus was the guest of honor in someone's home for dinner, and often he used these occasions to teach his hosts something of the Kingdom of God. For example, one evening he was having a meal in the palatial house of a conservative old, pillar-of-the-church type named Simon. There were swarms of servants milling around, and it was easy for an uninvited guest to slip in to the open court yard in the center of Simon's house. The guests were no doubt gathered about the pool, sort of semi-reclined on couches, which was the fashionable way to dine in those days. Eating around the swimming pool in our own time is nothing new. All at once there appeared a woman at Jesus' feet, one who was known to many of the guests as a woman of the streets. She was a prostitute, and hardly a welcome guest in the house of so pious a Pharisee as Simon.

Immediately her unwanted presence was brought to Simon's attention, but it was one of those awkward situations where he really did not know what to do. He was hesitant to create a scene and make a spectacle out of what might not amount to anything at all. On the other hand, if this Jesus was all the prophet he had heard he was, then intuitively, he would know this woman was immoral, and would order her out himself. So Simon decided to sit back and watch. Apparently the woman had heard that Jesus was there, and her own inner guilt and conflicts were driving her almost to the breaking point. With a boldness born of desperation, she risked everything to come to this pious house to seek out the young rabbi about whom she had heard so much.

And there she stood at the foot of his couch, overcome with emotion. Her plan was to wash the road dust off his feet with some fine soap she had saved, but suddenly, in her unsettled state of mind, she realized she had forgotten a towel. It was at that moment that she did something no respectable woman of her day would ever do in public. She unfastened her hair, letting it hang down to her shoulders, and then proceeded to dry the feet of Jesus with her hair. This exhibition was too much for Simon, who got up out of his seat, and hurried over to forcibly eject this intruder from his home. But Jesus stopped him.

"Simon," he said, "I know how you feel about this, and I have something I want to ask you." We can only imagine how the other guests must have stopped their eating and conversation. As a nervous hush settled over the dinner party, Jesus said, "Simon, if two men were in debt with a money lender, one for $500 and the other for $50, and neither could repay, and the lender let them off — which one of them do you suppose would be the most grateful?'' And Simon, wondering what this was all about, said, ''Well, I guess the one who had the biggest debt.''

Then Jesus said to him, ''That's absolutely right. What this woman does arises out of the depths of her heart because her many wrongs have been absolved. But, Simon, you have been forgiven little, and therefore, you love little.'' And then, turning to the woman herself, Jesus said, ''Your sins are forgiven; go in peace.'' That was Jesus Christ's gift to one woman — to all women — in fact, to every one of us. It is a gift of love and acceptance, no matter who, how, what, or where.

I thought of that woman and Jesus' gift of love when I ran across an old letter recently from a woman who wrote to me when I was first beginning at work as a pastor. Here is what she said: ''Dear Mr. Beringer, Four years ago I was married in your church and I know of nowhere else to turn. I want to know what you believe about divorce. My husband says that he still loves me, but I do not know whether I love him. I am sure I cannot stand living with him any longer. I have no one clear reason, but I can give you dozens of accumulated reasons which have piled up, and make it impossible for us to stay together. Please tell me what you think I should do.''

Now in those days I had all the answers, but thank God, he sometimes helps even those who in their sophomoric wisdom think they know it all! When I wrote back to the woman, I simply suggested that she make a careful list of all the things that she felt were making it impossible for the two of them to stay together. She did, and her dozens of accumulated reasons finally boiled down to eight complaints. Let me share her list with you:

1. He never takes me out any more. He just sits home watching football on the TV.
2. He pays more attention to the car than he does to me.

3. He never rinses the soap off after he uses it.

4. He always raves about his mother's cooking, but never says anything good about my meals.

5. When we are out with other people, he always talks about "my" house, "my" car, etc. He never uses the word "our."

6. He thinks I am stupid about money and refuses to open a joint checking account.

7. We have a fight every time I ask him to take me to see my folks.

8. The light in the cellar stairway has been burned out since last summer and I've asked him to fix it a hundred times, but he hasn't done it yet.

At the end of this list was appended a most interesting footnote, in which the writer admitted that all these so-called complaints sounded petty and unimportant. But she still asked about what she could do. Knowing I was already into a situation well over my head, I ran to the senior pastor with whom I was working for help. After reading the eight complaints, he handed the paper back to me and said, "Tell that couple to read 1 Corinthians 13 and let those words about love sink into their minds and hearts." That suggestion did not sound very profound to me, but I sat down and wrote another letter, this time including those familiar words from Paul's Epistle about love:

> Love is very patient, very kind. Love knows no jealousy, makes no parade, gives itself no airs, is never rude, never selfish, never irritated, never resentful. Love is never glad when others go wrong; love is satisfied by goodness, always slow to expose, always eager to believe the best, always hopeful and always patient.

Now there never was a better definition of genuine love, and each of the four characteristics that Paul lifts up for us about love is beautifully illustrated in Jesus' encounter with a sinful woman who experienced God's forgiveness. Let's examine each of those four qualities of love.

1. Patient Love

The love we see in Jesus' dealing with this woman is, first of all, a patient love. Only Jesus seems to have the patience to deal with a person whom others at this dinner party have judged and dismissed as being unimportant. It is no accident that when Paul describes genuine love, he puts "patience" first and last, for without patient understanding there is no love.

Many human relationships are lost without that quality of patient love. I smiled when I came across the story of the fellow who had returned to graduate school to get his doctorate. He found his wife was spending lonely evenings on a project of her own: writing a book about her experiences as a long-suffering wife of a grad student. The title of the book made it clear that she had not lost either her patience or her sense of humor. She called it, *What To Do Until The Doctorate Comes!"* Patient love as the Bible describes it is a willingness to accept the other person, faults and all. There surely is a real place for honesty and plain speaking in any good relationship, but I wonder if there is not also a time when harsh words spoken in anger might be better forgotten than spoken aloud. I can think of many a home that is intact today because some angry words were felt but never spoken aloud.

I once knew a woman who waited on her disagreeable and sick husband for seven long years. During that time she was rarely out of the house. She spent many sleepless nights sitting beside his bed; she grew frail and thin from denying herself. At the end of the seventh year, death claimed this man and he went to his eternal reward, free at last. But what I will never forget are the words of this wife, spoken to me after I had completed the funeral service. With not a trace of bitterness, she said to me, "Pastor, I have no regrets. I only thank the Lord for giving me the strength to care for him and to go on loving him until the end." That's patient love! It is a love that accepts another person, faults and all.

2. Kindly Love

A second quality we see in Jesus' dealing with this broken woman is kindly love. One can only imagine that this poor woman had experienced little kindness in her life. Most people related to her for what they could take from her, not what they could give. I think there is a deep hungering in many human hearts for a little kindness from those closest to us. Guy Lombardo, the famous band leader, used to tell of the time when he was given his first big chance to play over the radio from a Chicago dance hall. After the broadcast, Lombardo called his father in Ontario and asked him how he liked the show. "I heard you," said his father. "You were all right."

"Just all right? Weren't we great?" asked Guy Lombardo. "Look," said his father, "if it's compliments you want, I'll put your mother on the line!" Maybe that is why we idealize a mother's love — because often it is a mother's kindness that helps to soften the blows we all receive as children.

Perhaps this quality of kindness that we see so vividly illustrated in Jesus' dealing with a sinful woman is most missing in the most intimate relationships of life. A suave salesman will sing a smooth symphony to sell his product in the marketplace, but when he gets home, he addresses his wife and children in a voice that would clear a barnyard in thirty seconds! A man who was seventy-five years old went to his doctor for a checkup. The physician looked him over and said, "My friend, you are in perfect shape. I've never seen a man your age in better condition; tell me how you do it." The old man said, "Well, when my wife and I were married fifty-three years ago, we agreed that whenever I lost my temper, she would keep quiet and not answer back. And that whenever she lost her temper, I would take a walk. I suppose that my good health must be due to the fact that for the last fifty years, I've lived pretty much of an outdoor life!" Genuine love, the love we see in Jesus, is always a kindly love.

3. Unselfish Love

Still a third quality we see in Jesus is the unselfishness of his love. How easy it would have been to tell this woman to move along, for the Lord of heaven and earth was eating with important people that night. Instead, Jesus seems to forget completely about the danger to himself and his ministry, so completely absorbed is he in helping this woman to discover the forgiving and cleansing grace of God.

A friend of mine who is a Navy Chaplain tells of an occasion in the Pacific during the Second World War when the entire fleet turned from its course and formed a protective breakwater in rough seas so that emergency surgery could be performed aboard one ship in the middle of the fleet, and the life of one sailor saved. How unusual that is for those of us who live in the afterglow of the Me-Generation. We are more like admirals with such fleets under our command on the high seas of commerce and finance, clubs and fashions, and we would not think for a moment of turning aside our enterprises to save one human life. But Jesus did!

Again and again counselors tell us that the most precious of human relationships is destroyed by selfishness. At the counseling center in Marble Collegiate Church in New York, I am told they use the following technique to confront husbands and wives with unresolved bitterness in their relationship: They ask the man and the woman to sit alone in separate rooms with a ticking kitchen timer set for five minutes. During that period, they are asked to stop judging their marriage partner, and take a long look at themselves — to stand, as it were, in the other's shoes for those three hundred seconds and see themselves as others see them. This requires tremendous self-honesty, but for those who will open themselves to the process, it seems to work.

When one man came out of a session like this, he said, "After five minutes of really looking at myself from Helen's point of view, that clock's tick seemed awfully loud, and what it was saying was crystal clear. It pointed out the basic flaw in our marriage — my own preoccupation with *self, self, self.*"[1] The love we see in this tender story of our Lord's dealing with a broken life is a completely unselfish love, and it is a poignant illustration of Jesus' own words about "losing one's life in order to find it."

4. Forgiving Love

But what makes this one of the most beautiful of all stories in the Gospels is the quality of forgiving love we see in Christ. If any of us who have sinned and fallen far short of God's glory ever wondered if there is still a God who forgives, we need only remember this poor woman who dried Jesus' feet with her hair. Jesus gave that woman a gift that she did not deserve and could never earn — the gift of a clean slate before God, a second chance to live life as God intended. He gave her back her self-respect, and that is why forgiving love is a miracle of God's grace.

Recently I heard a true story that I know will haunt me for a long time. A young mother left her crawling, fourteen month old child unattended while she was doing laundry in the basement. The baby found some kind of cleaning compound, drank it all, and was dead on arrival at the hospital. The young mother sat there in the emergency room, stunned, stricken, waiting for her husband to come from work.

What would he say? He had idolized this child. When he did come, he took his wife in his arms, and said just five words: "My dearest, I love you!" Nothing else — no questions, no recriminations, no blame . . . just "My dearest, I love you." He put aside his own self-hurt, and did his best to draw the shelter of his love around their shared hurt.

That is the kind of forgiving love that Jesus once gave to a poor woman who crashed a fancy dinner party just to get near him. There were no questions, no recriminations, and no blame. Instead Jesus said to her, "Your faith has saved you;

go in peace.''

Do real people show love that is patient and kind, unselfish and forgiving? The answer is, they do — with the help of God's Holy Spirit at work in their hearts. By God's grace we can love one another in the same wonderful way that God has loved us in his Son, Jesus Christ.

Luke 9:18-24

Proper 7 (Common)
Pentecost 5 (Lutheran)
Ordinary Time 12 (Roman Catholic)

The Challenge That Tests One's Faith

Many years ago a somewhat stingy man decided to take a trip by stagecoach. He went to the ticket office and noticed that there were three different ticket prices for seats on the stage. There were first, second and third class tickets. But all the seats on the stagecoach looked the same to him, so he bought a cheaper, third class ticket and climbed aboard. The stage rolled along, and after awhile, the man was congratulating himself on his wisdom in purchasing a less expensive ticket. At that very moment, the stagecoach pulled up in front of a steep hill. The driver looked down at the passengers and shouted, "First class passengers may keep their seats. Second class passengers will get out and walk up the hill, and third class passengers will get out and push!"

Our text for this day has to do with what it means to be a "third class passenger" — that is, with the "get-out-and-push" aspects of what it means to be a follower of Jesus Christ. The fact is that you hear lots of sermons about the comfort and the benefits of being a Christian, but today we are going to talk about the costly demands of being a follower of Christ in a world like ours. Long ago, when I was in seminary, the faculty brought an executive from an advertising firm to talk to our class about how to be successful in ministry. As I remember his talk, he had two points: (1) If you want to increase church attendance, sing only the congregation's favorite hymns. (2) If you want the people to keep on coming, avoid such topics as crossbearing, the challenge of the faith, and the cost of discipleship. This sermon is prompted not by what we may *want* to hear but what I believe we *need* to hear about following Jesus Christ.

Art Linkletter interviewed children on television some years ago, asking them what they would write if they could prepare a letter to God. I recall one young boy saying he would write, "Dear God, count me in! Your friend, Joe." Joe was eight years old, but his magnificent promise lacked any awareness of the cost of being a disciple of Jesus Christ. The sad fact is that millions of adult members, hard-headed, critical-minded in worldly affairs, promise to follow Jesus Christ with little thought or understanding of what they are committing themselves to doing. When Jesus' disciples recognized him as the Christ of God, the first thing he did was to issue the challenge that tests our faith: "If anyone would come after me, let them deny themselves, take up the cross daily, and follow me." I have three questions to ponder with you as we consider that challenge.

1. Why Do We Need To Hear About Cost?

Why do we need to hear about the cost of being a Christian? One reason is that Jesus is a demanding Lord, and if we do not understand that, we do not understand him. It is characteristic of great leaders to make rigorous demands upon their followers. Joshua said to the people of Israel, "Choose you this day whom you will serve." Garibaldi in Italy offered his followers hunger and death — and Italy's freedom. Winston Churchill, as British Prime Minister in the dark days of the Second World War, promised his people "nothing but blood, toil, tears and sweat." Yet, in comparison, Jesus Christ was a thousand times more demanding than any of those great figures of history, Jesus Christ had no sympathy for people like the young woman of our own day who went to her doctor and said, "What can I do to feel better without giving up what is making me feel awful?"

By contrast it was Jesus who said, "Whoever does not renounce all that he has cannot be my disciple." Possessions cannot stand between the disciple and the Lord. Jesus said, "If anyone comes to me who doesn't hate his father and mother and wife and children and brothers and sisters for my sake, he cannot be my disciple." Not even family can stand between a disciple and the Lord. Jesus Christ demands our full obedience, and if we do not understand that, we simply do not understand him! Jesus is not some little wishy-washy Charlie Chaplin who comes to us with hat and cane in hand, hoping to win our favor and saying, "Please, may I have a word with you." Christ comes as the Lord of life and says, "Take up your Cross and follow me."

Still a second reason we need to hear about the cost and the challenge of being a Christian is that we are always in danger of falling for cheap grace. Nobody ever described the dangers of cheap grace more eloquently than Protestant theologian Dietrich Bonhoeffer who was hanged by Adolph Hitler in 1945, just before the liberation. Bonhoeffer was the one who said that cheap grace was the deadly enemy of the church. "Cheap grace means grace sold on the market like cheap Jack's wares. The sacraments, the forgiveness of sin, and the consolations of religion are thrown away at cut-rate prices."[1] Grace is represented as the church's inexhaustible treasury from which she showers blessings without ever asking questions or fixing limits. To be forgiven, no repentance is needed, and no change in one's daily life is expected. Cheap grace means comforting the afflicted without ever afflicting the comfortable. It is communion without confession and absolution without contrition. In short, it is the grace of God without the agonizing cross of Jesus Christ!

Now what does that mean for people like us? For professional clergy, it means that in our eagerness to attract people to the Christian enterprise, we have often underplayed the cost of being a Christian. We have too often preached about the consolations of the faith, but failed to remind our hearers about the demands of following Jesus Christ. For the television evangelists, our text raises the question, "Are you really telling your hearers and viewers about the cost of being a Christian?" You have in your hands the power to convince or deceive millions of people. You can persuade people that being a Christian is just as simple as kneeling in the living room and asking Christ to come to our lives. To be sure, the acceptance of Christ as Lord and Savior is the first step, but how many people are deceived into thinking that all one needs to do from then on is to send in a check every month to keep the evangelist's program on the air?

To the serious Christian our text suggests that there may well be areas of our lives where we have never let Jesus Christ enter. It is easy to proclaim that Christ is Lord of life and yet never allow him to rule your heart when you drive a car, or when you fill in your tax return, when you go out on a date, or when something sets off your miserable temper. To the not-so-serious Christian, our text says: "Don't confuse being socially acceptable or being a decent person with being a Christian. To be a follower of Jesus Christ is to be willing to bear any burdens he asks of you, to follow him into places you would never go, and to be willing to be laughed at, and even hurt for his sake." So all of us need to hear about the cost of being a Christian, because ours is a costly faith that has a cross at the heart of it.

2. How Shall We Understand Jesus' Challenge?

Here is a second question: How shall we understand Jesus' challenge to deny oneself and take up the cross when discipline is a dirty word and crosses are appointments on altars? What does it mean in our time to "deny oneself"? Does that mean a total abstinence from all of life's pleasures and joys? Some Christians have thought so, but I believe that Christ is talking about self-discipline in its most basic application to all of life. Fritz Kreisler, the virtuoso violinist, is reported to have said, "If I miss one day's practice, I know it. If I miss two days, my accompanist knows it; and if I miss three day's practice, the audience knows it." Vince Lombardi, winning coach of the Green Bay Packers for many years, declared flatly that the genius of effective coaching lies in drilling the players in the fundamentals of football — in short, self-discipline. Every profession, every human endeavor requires self-discipline, and God's venture to save this world from sin and death requires self-discipline and sacrifice on the part of those who follow Jesus Christ.

But let's be honest. In our narcissistic, hedonistic, materialistic culture, does not talk of self-discipline run contrary to the way most people think and live? The answer is an emphatic, "Yes." I remember hearing a gifted violinist play, and afterwards was present when someone from the audience said to the musician, "Oh that was wonderful! I would give my life to be able to play like that." The reply of the violinist said it all: "I *did* give my life."

Along with self-discipline, Jesus talks about taking up the cross. What in the world does that mean for Christians in America, people like us? I suggest that the sign of the cross in our time is sacrificial love. Such love is the only proper response in a world filled with oppressed, poverty-ridden, hungry people massed in Africa, Asia and in Latin America. It has been estimated that if the active Christians living in North America were to give just five percent of their material goods to ease the cruel hardships that crush the spirits of so many of the world's people, this turbulent world could be steadied and partially humanized and made just — by the impact of nothing more than sacrificial love! But the scandal of the church in our time is that we are content with a thin veneer of Christian love. We are members in good standing, but our concern for others is skin deep. We talk about the wondrous experience of meeting Christ on a Damascus Road but we are not willing to validate that experience by walking the Jericho Road with him, and reaching out in sacrificial love like the Good Samaritan to those who are hurting and dispossessed.

The Christ we follow is still saying, "Inasmuch as you did it to one of the least of these, you did it unto me." Praise God, there are Christians in every sphere of life who are willing to make that gift of sacrificial love to those in need. A few years ago at the Indianapolis Auto Race, a fine driver by the name of Al Unser skidded and hit the wall. He lay slumped in his burning car for only a few seconds before another racing vehicle skidded to a stop alongside his wrecked car. Then, while the other cars roared past with some coming dangerously close to the stopped cars, a young man, a deeply committed Christian by the name of Gary Bettenhausen, rushed over to Unser's car and began pulling the injured driver from the flames. Gary Bettenhausen had completely put out of his mind that he was in a race for which he had expended a fortune of money and many months of preparation. His only concern was the life of a man who surely would have burned to death. What a sacrifice.

Most of us have been moved by the stories of Mother Theresa's ministry in India. In the very first home that this Roman Catholic nun established, a man was brought in whose body was half-consumed by the ravages of cancer. A male attendant was overcome by the stench and turned away, retching. Mother Theresa took over the task herself. The miserable patient cursed her and said, "How can you stand the smell?" With a look of enormous compassion, the nun said quietly, "It's nothing to the pain you must feel." Jesus said, "If anyone would come after me, let them deny themselves, take up the cross daily and follow me."

3. Isn't Jesus Christ Asking Too Much?

Here is one final question: Honestly, isn't Jesus Christ asking too much of people like us? Isn't all this demand for self-discipline and sacrificial love more than any human being can promise? The answer is "Yes." It is more than any human being can promise on their own. If those first Christians had had to manage self-discipline, cross-bearing and obedient loyalty to Jesus in their own strength, they would have failed and faded from the pages of history.

What made the difference? The Risen Christ- who demanded so much wrapped that challenge in an amazing promise: "Lo, I am with you always, even unto the close of the age." In our own strength, we can never be the disciples Jesus Christ needs in this world. But we do not have to live the Christian life in our own strength! We walk in the power of his Holy Spirit. When we leave this place, we go out with a Christ beside us who helps us in our weakness, and who, by God's grace, helps us to become the men and women, the boys and girls God intended us to be. Many of you know and love the famous story of the Footprints In The Sand.

> I dreamed I was walking along the beach with the Lord and across the sky flashed scenes from my life. For each scene I noticed two sets of footprints in the sand. One belonged to me and the other to the Lord. But there came scenes when I noticed that there was only one set of footprints in the sand, and I noticed that they were the lowest and saddest times in my life. And so I questioned the Lord: Lord, you said you would walk with me all the way, yet in the darkest and most troublesome times in my life, I see only one set of footprints. Why would you leave me when I needed you the most? And the Lord answered, "My precious child, I would never leave you in your times of trial and suffering. When you see only one set of footprints in the sand, it was then that I carried you in my arms."[2]

Praise God for a Christ who is there to help us meet the challenge that tests our faith!

Luke 9:51-62

Proper 8 (Common)
Pentecost 6 (Lutheran)
Ordinary Time 13 (Roman Catholic)

Excuses

When it comes to matters of faith, people have always made excuses. Consider church attendance. Some claim they cannot come to church on Sunday because it is their only free day. They forget that it has been the church that kept the day free. Then there are those non-members who will not attend worship because they say, "All church members are hypocrites." I always like to invite people like that to church, not denying for a moment that we are often hypocritical in our walk of faith, but explaining that we always have room for one more in our church!

Each one of us, without too much effort, can manufacture excuses that could keep us from worship. At best, an excuse is a polite way out. It is a way of avoiding commitment and responsibility. An item in the paper caught my attention some years ago. The headline read, "No-Excuse Sunday Brings In The Sheep." It went on to tell how the Rev. Dale Barrick, in response to his parishioners' wide range of reasons for not attending services at the Great Hope Baptist Church in Carlisle, Pennsylvania, set up what he called "No-Excuse Sunday." It featured the following: cots for those who like to sleep in; blankets for those who found the sanctuary too cold; fans for those who found the sanctuary too warm; sand for those who preferred the beach; television sets for persons who prefer services on the screen; and poinsettias and lilies for those accustomed to entering the church only on Christmas and Easter.

Excuses are as old as the human family. Remember Adam, the father of the race, who rose to that first responsibility with an excuse, "the woman Thou gavest me, she gave me the fruit of the tree and I did eat." From that day on we have been making excuses to one another and to God for our behavior. Sometimes the excuses we offer are so ridiculous, they become laughable. One of our national magazines told the story of actor Mitch Ryan when they were making the film, *Magnum Force*. Ryan explained, "They had to postpone the scene in which I'm shot and killed." The cause of the postponement was set forth in a note from the company doctor to the director which said, "Mitch Ryan has a cold and is too sick to die today!"

But as ridiculous as some excuses we make to one another can get, excuses are serious business when it comes to our spiritual lives. By means of excuses, we can remain complacent, compromised and confused. Excuses fabricated for use by ourselves and prefabricated by our society, allow us to avoid the invitation of Jesus Christ to a life of discipleship and action. A lot of us continue to live on the premise that our excuses are valid. This is a delusion in itself, but worse yet, we think God is also taken in by our reasoning. The Scripture for this day describes the excuses offered by three would-be disciples of Jesus. However, their reasoning can give some insights into our own efforts to avoid commitment and responsibility. Let's look at each of them in turn.

1. Cost

The first man said, "Jesus, I will follow you anywhere." But to that magnificent offer, Jesus said, "Foxes have holes, birds have nests, but I am homeless." How discouraging an answer to such an enthusiastic admirer! We might well have expected Jesus to say, "Welcome aboard!" But Jesus Christ who knows the human heart so well, knew that this man was promising too much. He spoke the words of commitment, but he never bothered to count the cost. A lot of people were attracted to Jesus in his earthly ministry. It was the crowds, the healings, and the emotional impact of his presence that brought forth these weightless words of devotion. Words of infatuation are always useless. They are like firecrackers, spectacular for the moment, but then they return to earth as charred dust. Similarly, faith that demands nothing and costs nothing is usually worth nothing!

There are many persons in our own day who are still infatuated with Christianity as an easy way to obtain peace of mind, success, and even popularity. And Jesus is still asking us to count the cost of what it means to say, "I will follow you anywhere." The spiritual hucksters of our own time promise that for a mere smattering of prayer in a moment of crisis, we can experience the power of God. They portray heaven as an immense bargain basement (or attic) of spiritual reductions, where patience, humility, love, and all the fruits of the Spirit are available for next to nothing. To these people the cross of Christ is nothing more than a set of tricks and techniques for harnessing the power of God. The Christian faith in the presentation of many of these popular preachers is just a beneficial elective course in the success program of the world. How easily we forget that cheap grace produces cheap discipleship! We forget that Jesus told his followers to "deny themselves and take up the cross" before following him. Can it be that many of us are forced to make excuses in our discipleship, because we promised too much too soon?

When it comes to counting the cost, however, I find my problem is that I do little else but count the cost of following Christ. Often the church of our time hesitates so long before taking action that the response to Christ comes too late to be of any good. In a church newsletter that comes to our home, I read the following item called, "Conjectures Of A Bewildered Observer." Here is what it said:

86

Jesus said, "Follow me" but first we need a committee to review the work of the disciples.

Jesus said, "Follow me" but we need to evaluate the meaning of this statement — what is the intent?

Jesus said, "Follow me" but I question the results of such action — we could lose members and cause division.

Jesus said, "Follow me" but I think we should discuss this another time — the hours and days suggested are not convenient.

Jesus said, "Follow me" but I think we should, as a staff, write a paper and then we can react with more information.

Jesus said, "Follow me" but what will it cost in dollars? Our budget is already so tight.

Then a voice from heaven was heard: "For Jesus' sake and your own, just follow Him!"

—Robert E. Ryland[1]

Jesus Christ makes serious and complete demands upon our lives. He insists that we count the cost before promising to follow him. I believe we know in most cases what is involved in being Christ's disciple in this world, but we are not ready to go that far in faith.

2. Convenience

Jesus asked the next man to follow him. This man makes the commitment, but then seeks to delay acting on it. He says "Yes" to Christ, "Yes but later." How many of us are planning to accept and follow Christ later on? "I'll get religion when I get older" is the excuse we give ourselves. What we mean by that is, "When I am too feeble and weak to enjoy sinning, then I will consider religion." This man said to Jesus, "First let me go and bury my father." Now on the surface of it, that seems like an awfully good excuse. Most businesses today will grant employees an excused absence when there is a death in the family. However, there is nothing in the Bible that tells us this man is dead! What the would-be disciple is saying in effect is, "I have an aged father who is going to die sometime. When my responsibilities are over, then I will go with you." Unwilling minds never lack for an excuse!

There is much of this man in most of us. We want to be fellow travelers with Christ without the travel. We approve of Christ and we even want to side with him, but the world calls us back to our responsibilities. We feel we have to fulfill our obligations in life before we fulfill the call of God. "Jesus, I want to help you, but I can't do it just now." Is this not the same kind of excuse we offer in our own time? Have you ever said, "I am sorry I cannot teach in the church school, but I have so many obligations in the club this year"? "I am so busy with my children . . . couldn't you try me again?" In moments of clear honesty when we have put aside all the excuses, we can see that often our commitment is only verbal and in reality, we have not given ourselves to Jesus Christ.

The blunt fact is that we cannot make our worldly tasks an excuse for spiritual inactivity. God does not heed the request, "first my will and then yours, Lord." God wants the busy people of life, those for whom it would be all too easy to say, "Sorry Lord, I want to help you but it is just not convenient right now." Look at the persons God called to his service. The disciples were busy fishermen, Luke was a busy doctor, Lydia was a hard-working businesswoman, but these busy men and women were the ones God chose to become the backbone of his church. Being busy is no excuse for postponing our discipleship with Christ. Back in the early 1960s, I attended the presentation at Union Seminary in New York of a musical production entitled, *For Heaven's Sake*. One of the songs in that delightful musical was called "Use me, O Lord!" It was sung by a character called Cheerful Doer who, like the man who wanted to bury his father before following Jesus, was seeking some way of postponing his service until a more convenient time. Here is how the song goes:

As soon as I'm out of college,
And pay all the debts I've carried;
As soon as I've done my Army stint,
As soon as I've gotten married:

> *I want you to use me, Oh Lord,*
> *Use me, Oh Lord,*
> *But not just now . . .*

As soon as I get promoted
As soon as the house is built,
As soon as my psychiatrist
Says that I'm freed of guilt;

> *I want you to use me, Oh Lord,*
> *Use me, Oh Lord,*
> *But not just now . . .*

As soon as I've paid the mortgage,
As soon as the kids are grown;
As soon as they've finished college,
As soon as they're on their own;

> *I want you to use me, Oh Lord,*
> *Use me, Oh Lord,*
> *But not just now . . .*

As soon as I've reached retirement,
As soon as they're getting ahead;
As soon as I draw my pension,
Just as soon as I am dead!

> *I want you to use me, Oh Lord,*
> *Use me, Oh Lord,*
> *But not just now . . .*[2]

Jesus said, "Let the dead bury the dead." Let the world be primarily concerned with the tasks of the world. You who have accepted me are called out of the world to do my work in the

Kingdom. The world will take care of its own business. The question is, who will spread the Gospel, who will do my work? Let the dead bury the dead that you, the living, might speak the words of life.

3. Conflicting Loyalties

To the challenge, "Follow me," the third man answers, "First let me go and say goodbye." This is the response of a person with conflicting loyalties. When people linger long and repeat often the word, "goodbye," you can be sure they do not want to go. How many times does a young couple say goodbye on the doorstep, so as to avoid the moment of parting?

To go back is to go into temptation. The people at home could change the commitment of this would-be disciple. They could say to him, "Don't be a fanatic. Maybe this Jesus is the Messiah and maybe not. Don't go rushing off to follow him. Wait awhile. Too much religion can be a dangerous thing." When we go back to the old places of life, we carry on a flirtation with the very things from which Christ calls us. Jesus Christ expects a person to leave the old life in order to gain a whole new life in him. Recall the Old Testament story of Lot's wife. She took a last, long, lingering took at the old life and it encased her. She went from mortal to monument in the moment of looking back.

Some of us are carrying on the same kind of flirtation with the ways of this world. The hankering to do what the world does and still profess Christ is the human spirit looking back. To look back is to draw back; to draw back is to hold back; and to hold back is like the kiss of Judas. Holding back is an outward sign of acceptance, that is, the kiss — while the basic motive is rejection. We are playing a dangerous game when we try to be both for and against Christ, according to the situation in which we find ourselves.

If we are to move beyond excuses in our walk of faith, we

must understand once and for all that Jesus demands prima-
cy. God never settles for second place and he never offers you
and me the second best. His will must be first, his tasks first,
his kingdom first, and then all the rest of life will fall into its
proper order. To put it another way, Jesus Christ did not give
his life on a cross for a once-in-a-while, compartmentalized,
when-it's-convenient sort of faith. The quality of our commitment to Christ must be guided by the quality of his commitment to us, which is total! Jesus Christ wants to be the
controlling factor in your life. He wants you and me to surrender our wills and our gifts to him, so that he can weave
our lives into the fabric of his purpose for this world. To make
the ultimate surrender is to know the very power and presence
of Jesus Christ at work in your life.

Albert Schweitzer, son of a German Lutheran pastor, brilliant, exceptionally talented, extraordinarily gifted, and well-
educated, could have gone anywhere with any career of his
choosing, be it medicine, philosophy, music, or theology. In
a sense, Europe was at his disposal. But then he says, "While
at the university and enjoying the happiness of being able to
study and even to produce some results in science and art, I
could not help but think continually of others for whom Jesus died, who were denied that happiness by their material cir-
cumstances or their health. Then one brilliant summer morning
at Gunsbach, during the Whitsuntide holidays — it was in 1896
— there came to me as I awoke, the thought that I must give
something in return for it."[3] Subsequently, Schweitzer decided to take all of his gifts and use them for the glory of Jesus
Christ as a medical missionary.

We may not have all the gifts and endowments of Albert
Schweitzer, but the call of Christ comes to each one of us to
lay aside our excuses, and to give ourselves — heart, mind,
and soul — to follow him. In the Book of Hebrews we read
these words:

> Therefore, since we are surrounded by so great a cloud of witness-
> es, let us lay aside (put off) every weight, (every hindrance), and

every sin which clings so closely and run the race that is set before us, looking to Jesus, the pioneer and perfecter of our faith.

Beloved in Christ, let us lay aside our excuses! I challenge you, with Christ's help, to concentrate on that great race which is set before us!

Luke 10:1-12, 17-20 [C, RC]
Luke 10:1-12, 16 (17-20) [L]

Proper 9 (Common)
Pentecost 7 (Lutheran)
Ordinary Time 14 (Roman Catholic)

Power To The People

In one of our church magazines appeared an article about religious language. There we learn that the word "meaningful" is now out and the word "powerful" is now in! In the 1970s, people yearned for a "meaningful relationship." They wanted "meaningful worship" in their churches on Sunday. They were willing to enter into "meaningful dialogue" and they told one another to read books that were "particularly meaningful" to them.

But suddenly, "meaningful" is out. Today's word is "powerful." When a pastor is really speaking to the hearts of people, they say it was a "powerful sermon." People seem to hunger for what they describe as "powerful worship experiences." They want to share "powerful ideas" with one another. More often in the business world than in the church, people speak about having had a "power lunch." Now I confess I do not know what a "power lunch" is, but I certainly would love to have one!

All this talk about power suggests that many Christians are feeling "powerless" in their walk of faith, and that many of our churches feel as if their witness in the modern world counts for almost nothing. In the same journal where we read about changes in religious language, the very next article was entitled, "How To Recover Presbyterian Power." Many Christians get discouraged in our time, because it seems that the forces

that really move life in this world are the forces of material-
ism, secularism, humanism, the fanatical faith of Islam, or
the more familiar gods of money, power and pleasure. Who
really expects the church to make any real difference in the
life of this world? That's great material for Sunday sermons
. . . but who really takes it seriously on Monday morning?

For many persons today, the church is simply a *chaplain's
office*. It is a place to go when you are in trouble or when you
need help with a baptism, a wedding, or a funeral. For those
folks, the church is simply a place where you get hatched,
matched, and dispatched!

For others, the church is more like a *country club* than anything else. You pay your dues and then enjoy the privileges.
A former Moderator of the General Assembly of the Presbyterian Church, after having finished his year of touring
throughout the churches of America, wrote these words:

> The average Presbyterian Church is a fellowship of middle class
> people who enjoy being affiliated with an organization of good
> standing in the community, to which they can belong with comfort
> and without too great expense, who believe in brotherhood within
> well-defined limits, most of whom cast a conservative vote, and who
> find satisfaction in listening to short sermons and tolerable church
> music, and in being associated with respectable people of their own
> class.[1]

What that former church official describes is a country club,
and for many people in our time, that is all the church really
seems to be.

Still others in our day, wanting the church to be a powerful voice in society, seem to have concluded that the church
must become a *political party* in order to be effective. These
are the voices of almost every church in America who believe
that the only way to change people and nations is the political
way. They have sought to be relevant by having the churches
make social pronouncements on almost every issue known to
the human mind. For them, the name of the game is econom-

ic and political power! While most Christians readily agree that the church should take a stand on moral issues, the result of this politicization of the church has been the mass exodus of thousands of people who think of the church as a cut flower, an institution that will not bloom much longer because it is divorced from its biblical and spiritual roots.

Among both Roman Catholic and Protestant Christians, there are many voices calling for spiritual renewal, but it is not likely that the church of our time will find that kind of spiritual re-awakening in hard-sell evangelism, in more social action or in some sort of gigantic ecumenical merger. The future of the church would seem to rest in our ability to recover the ministry that Jesus Christ began on this earth nearly two thousand years ago. The church exists only through Christ, and it must recommit itself to Christ if we are to be anything more than sound and fury, signifying nothing! The ministry of Jesus was one that put persons first, not programs, principals, institutions, or even success. Jesus began with a few changed lives, and those changed persons moved out into a hostile society, radiating the power, the love, and the grace of God they have found in Jesus. They incarnated divine truth and love in their very lives, and they changed the world, not by social pronouncements, but by spiritual power from the transcendent Lord. Luke's account of the sending forth of the seventy gives us an excellent illustration of how the ministry of Jesus released the power of God through ordinary people with amazing results.

1. Enabling The Few

Jesus Christ built his Kingdom by enabling the few. "Every time I look at you, I don't understand," cries the voice of Judas Iscariot in the rock opera, *Jesus Christ Superstar*. What Judas does not understand is how Jesus Christ chose to manage his ministry! To him, it was badly planned, badly timed, and badly placed. Why could not Jesus have waited a couple millenia, and have chosen to use mass communication? What Jesus needed was a public relations department who could handle the television rights, the beer commercials, and the political organization!

But that is the point. Jesus Christ chose not to operate on the grand scale and to start a popular movement. He came to inaugurate the Kingdom of God, God's righteous rule, in human hearts and in society, and he made it crystal clear that this Kingdom begins on the small scale, like a pebble dropped into a lake with ever widening ripples. In fact, Jesus began with just four fishermen whom he called beside the Sea of Galilee. You just can't start much smaller than that! Later he enlarged the group to twelve. Finally he sent out seventy men and women to extend his ministry into the surrounding towns and villages. That was his method, *to enable the few*. He rejected mass communication in favor of training a few dedicated disciples who would be the link with his ongoing kingdom.

Did it work? Well, according to Luke it was so stunningly successful that when the seventy returned, Jesus said with great joy, "I saw Satan fall like lightning from heaven." In other words, here was a method that would eventually win, a strategy that the forces of evil could not withstand, a church against which the gates of hell could not prevail.

At the funeral of Sir Winston Churchill, the procession was headed by a single rank of middle aged men wearing the faded uniforms of the Royal Air Force. They were all that remained of the few hundred young Englishmen flying small fighter aircraft who beat back the German Luftwaffe in 1940. Churchill himself paid them a great tribute when he said, "Never . . . was so much owed by so many to so few."[2] I would like to think that when the saints march into heaven, the procession will be headed by a group of men fresh from their Galilean fishing boats, and later generations at the end of the great procession will say of them, "Never was so much owed by so many to so few." Jesus Christ began by enabling the few to reach the many.

2. He Sent Them Out

Our Lord's second strategy was to send out those whom he had trained to preach the Kingdom of God and to heal the sick. Without much warning and without too much training, Jesus sent the seventy to go ahead of him. We know almost nothing of these seventy men and women. Presumably not a one of them was a graduate of a theological seminary! The Scriptures tell us they were sent out to be *heralds* of the new Kingdom. I find this enormously suggestive for what we Christians of the 1980s are called to be. These seventy disciples were not to impose their customs or dietary laws on anyone. They were not sent out to announce personal values or to set up organizations or even to run programs. They were essentially sent out to tell the good news that in Jesus Christ, God has come to redeem his people from their sins. I am convinced that we have made being a Christian a bigger assignment than it really is. With all our talk about evangelism, about mission, and about ministry, I sometimes think the average person in the church today does not feel qualified to do any of it. We have made the most basic activity of the church, that of sharing the good news of Jesus Christ, seem so intimidating that most people are scared to death to do it!

Perhaps that is why we have become a church with a minority of participants and a majority of observers. We think we cannot function as a church unless the religious professionals are there to show us what to do. I smiled some weeks ago when I read about a tiny mission church in Alaska that was seeking a new pastor. A committee was formed, contacts were made with the Mission Board back in New York City, but months went by and not a single candidate was sent out by the Board to be interviewed. Finally, in frustration, the chairperson of the committee sent a telegram to the Mission Board in New York which read: "Forget the minister. We've found sinning is more fun!'' The new pastor arrived in just two weeks!

Jesus Christ never intended those he sent out to be theologically trained specialists. He simply wanted heralds of Good News. Do you recall the story of how Karl Barth, the most gifted theologian of the 20th Century, was asked to sum up his faith in one sentence? The great theologian, who had written volumes of books, paused for a moment and then said that his theology could be summed up in the words of a song his mother sang to him each night at bedtime. It was, ''Jesus loves me, this I know, for the Bible tells me so.'' That is what we believe, and that is what we are called to live out, and that is what we are sent out into the world to share with others!

3. Promise Of Power

But Jesus did more than send out a select few persons. He promised them nothing less than the power of God in their ministry. The awesome power that Jesus conferred on the seventy was spiritual power. But the moment we begin to talk about spiritual power in the modern world, many will turn away. For them the only power that counts is economic power, military power or political power — or even the power of one's own personal influence. Still, the world is beginning to recognize that there is another kind of power. It is a power that persuades, as in the case of Ghandi. It is a power that will lead one to make incredible sacrifices, as evidenced in the life of Mother Theresa. It is a power that comes through faith. Christians believe that it is the power of the Spirit of God dwelling in the heart that empowers us to be the heralds of Christ in this world.

One thinks of Terry Waite, the Anglican Envoy. This imposing man of 6'7" was, until his imprisonment, trying to gain the release of hostages in Lebanon. Terry Waite operated with no more power than the power of moral and spiritual persuasion. He appealed to the Shi'ite Muslims who are holding their hostages on spiritual grounds. He had no trump card, no army to let loose, no threats to make. But that is the same sort of power that Jesus Christ gives to his followers in every age. It is a power that works from within, a power that appeals to the heart as well as to the mind, and a power that is greater than human strength and human wisdom.

How do we get this power? *We ask for it!* Think of the television commercials for the investment firm of Smith Barney. The man says, "We make money the old-fashioned way — we *earn* it!" We can find the power of God for our lives the old-fashioned way — *we ask for it*! One day a small boy tried to lift a heavy stone but couldn't budge it. His father, watching, finally said, "Are you sure you're using *all* your strength?" "Yes, I am," the boy cried. "No, you are not," said the father quietly, "you haven't asked me to help you yet." Many of us have never tasted the promised power of Jesus in our walk of faith because we have never asked our Heavenly Father to help us with his power. When the seventy asked for that power, they returned saying, "Lord, even the demons are subject to us in your name!"

4. Returned With Joy

But what were the results of this mission of the seventy? Luke tells us that the Seventy returned with joy. Too often when you and I think about the Christian life, we forget that our Lord intended us to live it in joy. Sometimes sermons that call us to a life of discipleship and service seem about as much fun as a low-fat, low-salt, low-everything diet! The image many people still have of the Christian life is represented by the little fellow who, because it was Sunday, could not play with friends, or with toys, or do anything that was fun. Because he lived on a farm, he wandered down into the pasture behind his house where he saw a mule with a long, sad face, standing by the fence. The little boy went up to the mule, patted his nose and said, "Poor fellow . . . you must be a Christian too!"

This ministry that our Lord Jesus Christ committed to us

is not some joyless task. It is meant to be a joyous adventure of faith. As we experience his power and his grace here in worship, and then go forth to share his love with the world, we too will experience a joy that nothing in all this world can ever take away.

There was once a visitor to an African mission station who watched as a missionary nurse dressed the ugly sores of a leper. The stench was terrible and when the nurse had finished, the visitor said to her, "I wouldn't do what you have just done for a million dollars!" He was surprised when the nurse turned and said to him, "Neither would I for a million dollars, but I do it every day gladly for my Savior Jesus Christ.

Let us go forth in *joy* to serve the Lord!

Notes

Introduction

1.   Quoted by C. Thomas Hilton, *Master Sermon Series*, July 1986, Cathedral Publishers, Royal Oak, Michigan, Page 350.

Promises, Promises

1.   A. Leonard Griffith, *The Eternal Legacy From An Upper Room,* Harper and Row, New York, 1963, Page 97. Used by permission.

2.   Ted Husing, "I Could Not Hide From My Friends," published in *Guideposts,* Carmel, N.Y., April, 1960.

3.   A. Leonard Griffith, *What Is A Christian?*, Abingdon Press, Nashville, Tennessee, 1962, Page 191. Used by permission.

4.   Quoted by C. Thomas Hilton, *Master Sermon Series*, July 1986, Cathedral Publishers, Royal Oak, Michigan, Page 352.

Help Available

1.   Catherine Marshall, *The Helper,* Avon Books, New York, 1978, Page 32. Used by permission.

2.   A. Leonard Griffith, *God's Time and Ours*, Abingdon Press, Nashville, Tennessee, 1964, Page 146. Used by permission.

3.   Ernest Gordon, *Through The Valley Of The Kwai*, Harper and Row, New York, 1962, Page 174. Used by permission.

The Wind Of God

1.   Quoted in a sermon by Dr. Robert C. Holland, Shadyside Presbyterian Church, Pittsburgh, Pennsylvania, January 21, 1973. Used by permission.

Where Do We Find God?

1.   A. Leonard Griffith, *God's Time and Ours*, Abingdon Press, Nashville, Tennessee, 1964, Page 148. Used by permission.

Making A Lot Out Of A Little

1. A. Leonard Griffith, *God's Time And Ours*, Abingdon Press, Nashville, Tennessee, 1964, Pages 199-200. Used by permission.

2. William Barclay, *And He Had Compassion On Them,* The Church of Scotland Youth Committee, Edinburgh, Scotland, 1966, Page 165. Used by permission.

3. William Barclay, *And He Had Compassion On Them*, The Church Of Scotland Youth Committee, Edinburgh, Scotland, 1966, Page 168. Used by permission.

The Outsider

1. A. Leonard Griffith, *What is a Christian?,* Abingdon Press, Nashville, Tennessee, 1962, Page 114. Used by permission.

2. A. Leonard Griffith, *What is a Christian?,* Abingdon Press, Nashville, Tennessee, 1962, Page 118. Used by permission.

3. Edith Gittings Reid, *The Great Physician*, Oxford University Press, New York, 1931, Page 56. Used by permission.

4. Charles W. Colson, *Born Again*, Bantam Books, New York and London, 1976, Page 144. Used by permission.

Making People Whole

1. A. Leonard Griffith, *We Have This Ministry,* Word Books, Waco, Texas, 1973, Page 93. Used by permission.

2. William Barclay, *And He Had Compassion On Them,* The Church of Scotland Youth Committee, Edinburgh, Scotland, 1966, Page 130.

3. As told by Dr. Norman Vincent Peale in his monthly magazine, *Creative Help for Daily Living,* February, 1974.

4. As quoted in a Hartford, Connecticut Newspaper in January, 1987.

By The Hair Of A Sinner

1. Quoted in a sermon delivered by Dr. Robert C. Holland in the Church-On-The-Green, Morristown, New Jersey, on February 14, 1971.

The Challenge That Tests One's Faith

1. Dietrich Bonhoeffer, *The Cost Of Discipleship,* Macmillan Company, New York, 1949, Page 38. Used by permission.

2. Reprinted by permission of Antioch Publishing Company, Yellow Springs, Ohio.

Excuses

1. Quoted in the newsletter of the Whitworth Presbyterian Church, Spokane, Washington, March 1987.

2. Helen L. Kromer, *For Heaven's Sake*, Baker's Plays, Boston, Massachusetts, 1961, Pages 37-39. Used by permission.

3. Maurice A. Fetty, *Putting Your Life On The Line*, Abingdon Press, Nashville, Tennessee, 1977, Page 33. Used by permission.

Power To The People

1. Quoted from remarks made by Wilbur LaRoe following his year as Moderator of the General Assembly of the United Presbyterian Church in the U.S.A., 1958.

2. A. Leonard Griffith, *We Have This Ministry,* Word Books, Waco, Texas, 1973, Page 73. Used by permission.

About the Author

Robert Beringer is a native of New Jersey and has spent his entire ministry of nearly thirty years in the Garden State. Having begun his college work at Cornell University in the field of hotel administration, he felt a strong call to ministry while working as a volunteer in several churches in upstate New York. Following graduation, he enrolled in Princeton Theological Seminary where he obtained a Bachelor of Divinity Degree in 1961. His first position after seminary was in Bound Brook, New Jersey where he was called as associate pastor. In 1964 he became the pastor of the First Presbyterian Church of Hopewell, New Jersey where he served for the next twenty years. In the summer of 1984, Bob moved to Metuchen where he is currently the head of staff in a parish of 1100 members in a suburb of New York City.

Throughout his ministry, Bob has been active in his denomination, having served as moderator of New Brunswick Presbytery in 1970. He currently chairs the Committee On Ministry of Elizabeth Presbytery, and has chaired comittees on Christian education, social witness, evangelism, candidates, and vocation.

In the wider community Bob has chaired the board of a local Family Service Association, served for many years on the Board of the Campus Ministry at Rutgers University, served for many years on the Board of the Campus Ministry at Rutgers University, and has chaired the Board of Trustees for the Presbyterian Homes of New Jersey in a ministry that includes some 1600 residents. In addition he is Past Master in the Masonic Lodge and has participated in the work of local rescue squads. For many years he served on a Juvenile Conference Committee as an arm of the Juvenile Court in New Jersey.

Bob is married to Margaret Chamberlain Beringer. He and Peggy are the parents of four adult children. He is the author of *The Easter People,''* also published by the C.S.S. Publishing Company.